Hildebrand Bowman

The Travels of Hildebrand Bowman, Esquire

Into Carnovirria, Taupiniera, Olfactaria, and Auditante, in New-Zealand

Hildebrand Bowman

The Travels of Hildebrand Bowman, Esquire
Into Carnovirria, Taupiniera, Olfactaria, and Auditante, in New-Zealand

ISBN/EAN: 9783337184339

Printed in Europe, USA, Canada, Australia, Japan

Cover: Foto ©Andreas Hilbeck / pixelio.de

More available books at **www.hansebooks.com**

THE
TRAVELS

OF

HILDEBRAND BOWMAN,

ESQUIRE,

Into CARNOVIRRIA, TAUPINIERA, OLFACTARIA, and AUDITANTE, in NEW-ZEALAND; in the Ifland of BONHOMMICA, and in the powerful Kingdom of LUXO-VOLUPTO, on the GREAT SOUTHERN CONTINENT.

WRITTEN by HIMSELF;

Who went on fhore in the ADVENTURE's large Cutter, at Queen Charlotte's Sound New-Zealand, the fatal 17th of December 1773; and efcaped being cut off, and devoured, with the reft of the Boat's crew, by happening to be a-fhooting in the woods; where he was afterwards unfortunately left behind by the ADVENTURE.

An Ape, and Savage (cavil all you can),
Differ not more, than Man compared with Man.
ANONYMOUS.

LONDON:
Printed for W. STRAHAN; and T. CADELL, in the Strand. 1778.

TO

JOSEPH BANKS, Esq.

AND

DANIEL CHARLES SOLANDER,
M. D. LL. D.

GENTLEMEN,

I ADDRESS these *Travels* to you, as the best judges of the veracity of some part of them; and as my friend *Omai* was indebted to your friendship and protection (before you could possibly discover his intrinsic merit), to the grateful remembrance of *favours* received in his native country; I flatter myself, you will not refuse your Patronage to one, who was adopted into a Nation, with whom you held

a friendly

DEDICATION.

a friendly intercourfe in the *Southern Hemifphere*, becaufe he was born in *England*.

The inhabitants of great part of *New-Zealand*, are certainly much lefs civilifed than thofe of *Otaheite* and the other *Paphian* Ifles; but had you been fortunate enough to have fallen in with the *Auditantine* coaft, and could have converfed with the natives, I make no doubt but the fair *Shepherdeffes* of that country, would have rivalled your favourite *charmers*, with this advantage, they fcorn all *pilfering*, but that of *hearts*.

Should *Government* think proper to fend any *fhips* to cultivate *friendfhip* and *commerce* with the Nations I have difcovered, and I am honoured with the command of one of them, nothing

DEDICATION.

thing could add so much to my satisfaction on that event, as the company of two *Gentlemen*, who have set so laudable an example to all the European *Literati*, of braving the greatest dangers in the pursuit of useful knowledge.

I have the honour to be, with profound respect,

GENTLEMEN,

Your most devoted,

humble Servant,

St. Alban's-Street,
March, 20th, 1778.

HILDEBRAND BOWMAN.

A CARD.

Mr. Bowman presents his respectful compliments to the *Public*, and hopes they will not expect from one of his education and profession, purity of style, or correctness of composition. To these pleasing and elegant parts of *writing*, these high finishings, he makes no pretension; but in this *Narrative*, contents himself with a simple relation of facts; valuable only for an inviolable adherence to *truth*, without disguise and without ornament.

He flatters himself, some allowances will be made for the *Plates*, when it is observed, that they were *drawn* and etched by himself. His talents

talents in *Design* (though useful to him in his *Travels*), he is conscious are below mediocrity; and that these specimens now published, require an apology for their appearance in this country at present, when it abounds with excellent *Artists*. What he begs leave to say in excuse is, that one of moderate abilities in the *art*, might possibly represent a scene, in which he had been interested, either as a *spectator* or *actor*, with more *truth*, than another of superior merit could be able to do, only from meer description.

THE CONTENTS.

CHAP. I.

THE Author's birth, and education. His entering into the Navy. Admitted on board the Adventure as a Midshipman. Voyage to the South-Seas. Visits New-Zealand, Outaheite, and other Islands. The Adventure separated from the Resolution. Returns to New-Zealand, where the large Cutter and her Crew are cut off by the Cannibals. The Author escapes, and after wandering long in search of the Ship, sees her under sail, and out of his reach. Gets a-cross a Strait in a Canoe, into the Country of the Taupinicrans. Page 1

CHAP.

CONTENTS.

CHAP. II.

The miserable condition of the Author in Taupiniera. An account of that extraordinary People. Page 40

CHAP. III.

Arrives in Olfactaria. Is adopted by that Nation. Marries. Irruption of the Carnovirrians. Conclusion of that War, The Author elected a Chief of the Third, Second, and First Orders. His ammunition exhausted, and he in fear of being degraded, from his want of practice with their weapons, as well as of a nose. Gets the command of a large Canoe going to Auditante, to exchange their Skins. Arrives at Seripante. 78

CHAP.

CONTENTS.

CHAP. IV.

Seripante a Factory of Bonhommican Merchants. The Author and his Collegues live at their houses. Very fair Traders. Visit the Tents of the Natives. He learns in a short time the Bonhommican and Auditantine languages. Makes a speech to the Olfactarian Chiefs at taking leave of them. By invitation lives sometime at a Horde of the Auditantines. Falls in love. Lucky discovery which cures him of it. The Fleet from Ludorow arrives. The Fair held in consequence of it. The Author embarks in it, on its return. Arrives at Ludorow. Page 117

CHAP. V.

The Author invited to reside with a near relation of his friend at Seripante. By the means of him, and others to whom he had

had letters, he is presented to the Lord Admiral, to the Lord Treasurer, and at last to the Queen. She settles a pension on him. He confers with Officers, Astronomers, Surveyors, Physicians, and Mechanics, on the means of introducing the English improvements into the Bonhommican Navy. He is appointed a Post Captain, and is to command a ship of forty guns (going to the southern continent), under a Commodore. Has the fitting her out in the English manner. She is much admired. The Queen dines on board of her. They sail for Luxovolupto. Arrive safely at Mirovolante.

Page 165

CHAP. VI.

A Description of the Island of Bonhommica and its Inhabitants. Their Moral Sense.

CONTENTS. xiii

Senſe. Manners. Cuſtoms. Laws. Government. Religion, &c. &c.
Page 210

CHAP. VII.

The Commanders of the Ships of War invited to lie at the Merchants houſes of the Bonhommican Factory at Mirovolante. Of the pretended ſuperiority of the Luxo-voluptans in the ſenſe of Taſte. Commonneſs of Wheel Carriages in Mirovolante. A wonderful Stigma on failures in Chaſtity of both ſexes. Sees Garrimond, a famous Actor, in one of Avonſwan's Plays. The Commanders introduced at Court. The Author ſought after by the Nobility as coming from a far country. Balls. Routs. Concerts. A Maſquerade. Moraveres taken ill. Practice of Phyſic. State of Luxo-volupto, and neighbouring Kingdoms. The Bonhommican

CONTENTS.

mican sailors mobbed on a rejoicing night for the election of a Patriot. Page 253

CHAP. VIII.

Law. A Criminal Trial. Some account of the Country. Miro-volante. Army. Fleet. Manufactures. Court. Dress. Language. Learning. Hospitals. Summer Amusements. Summer Theatre. Rondelleva. Fairy Hall. Horse Race. 320

CHAP. IX.

Every thing prepared for sailing. Take leave at Court; and of our Friends. Sail with a fair wind. Speak with some Armoserian Privateers. A Storm. Meet with a Dutch Frigate. The Captain of her gives the Author a passage to Batavia. Tender parting with Moraveres.

raveres. His friendly behaviour to the Author; and humanity to the Dutch Crew. The Scurvy abates on board the Harlem Frigate, from the use of Malt and other things Moraveres spared them. Arrives at Batavia. Sent for by the Governor and Council, to interrogate him concerning the Island of Bonhommica. Ships fitted out for that discovery. The Author falls sick, but recovers. Sails to the Cape in a Dutch Indiaman. Gets a passage home in an English one. Arrives in Old England. **Page 372**

ERRATA.

Page 173. *line* 8. *read* opulence.
     239. *line* 17. *read* Anjouvini.
     266. *line* 19. *read* would do.
     278. *line* 19. *dele* are.
     328. *line* 18. *for* or *read* of.
     346. *line* 2. *read* in a medium.

THE
TRAVELS
OF
Hildebrand Bowman, Efq.

CHAP. I.

The Author's birth, and education. His entering into the Navy. Admitted on board the Adventure as a Midshipman. Voyage to the south Seas. Visits New Zealand, Otaheite, and other Islands. The Adventure separated from the Resolution. Returns to New Zealand, where the large Cutter and her Crew are cut off by the Cannibals. The Author escapes, and after wandering long in search of the ship, sees her under sail, and out of his reach. Gets across a Strait in a Canoe, into the Country of the Taupinierans.

I Was born in Holderness, a district of Yorkshire, near the Borough of Heyden; of which my Father was a free-a freeman. He was a man of great probity and induſtry in buſineſs, and had acquired a competent fortune by farming. A conſiderable farm of Squire Conſtable's, and a ſmaller of his own inheritance, were occupied by him. His family was large; conſiſting of four ſons, and three daughters: of all of us he was equally fond, and ſpared no money on our education, according to his notions of things. I was the third of his ſons in order of birth, and we were all taught to read Engliſh by our Mother, who was a very pious worthy woman. My Father alſo ſometimes heard us ſay our leſſons, and inſtilled early into our minds, the love of honeſty and truth. Theſe repeated inſtructions of his, made a deep impreſſion on mine; to ſo great a degree, that I have always ſcrupulouſly adhered to truth, even in the moſt indifferent matters.

When

When I was eight years old, my Father fent my brother James (who was a year older) and me, to Pocklington grammar-fchool, which was then in confiderable reputation in that country. I foon became a kind of favourite, both of the Mafter and the Ufher's, from my good behaviour; not that I wanted fprightlinefs, or was not fometimes caught in unlucky tricks, like others of my age, but they were generally overlooked, as they never found me deviating from truth. But what greatly contributed alfo to it was, that I had a great facility in learning languages, and confequently was, what is called, a good fcholar. This talent has been of great advantage to me in my travels.

I was taken from fchool at fifteen years old, having gone through that part of my education with fome applaufe;

plaufe; and my Father defired me to confider maturèly, what way of life would be moſt agreeable to my inclinations; as he was refolved to indulge his children in every thing which would not tend to their own detriment.

Having been born within a few miles of Hull, a confiderable fea-port; and by that means having frequent opportunities of feeing fhips of all kinds; as well as of hearing of the different countries to which they traded; I conceived an early partiality for that way of life, which was ſtrengthened and confirmed by reading books of Voyages and Travels, whenever I could meet with them. When I made this known to my Father, he did not oppofe it; but as boys often conceive very falfe and inadequate notions of things, he refolved to fend me a fhort voyage by way of trial, before my deſtination

was

was absolutely fixed. A ship was going from Hull to the whale fishery; and, at my desire, that voyage was fixed on. And as there remained five or six months to be disposed of before she would sail, I was sent to that town to learn Mathematicks, Navigation, the French language, Dancing, and Drawing. Having a good ear and being fond of music, I also made some proficiency on the German Flute. My voyage to Greenland was very far from putting me out of conceit with a sea-life, and my Father had some thoughts of binding me apprentice to a Master of a ship of his acquaintance at Hull. But some of his friends represented to him, that having such a friend in the Navy as the worthy member for Heyden, Sir Charles Saunders, it would be a pity to stint the boy's genius, who probably might make

make a figure in the King's fervice, and become an Admiral himfelf in time. This pleafed my little ambition too much, not to prefs my Father to confent; who, unwilling to baulk me in what was no way blameable, wrote to Sir Charles concerning it; defiring, if he approved of the fcheme, to favour him with his intereft in placing me properly. He received an anfwer in ten days, defiring I might be immediately fent to London, as he approved of my going into his Majefty's fervice. When I waited on him, he afked me a great many queftions, with a defign I fuppofe to try my genius; and feemed pleafed with my anfwers. It being at that time a profound peace in the weftern parts of Europe, few fhips of war were in commiffion, and it required good intereft to procure a birth. But he very foon informed

formed me, that Captain Narbury, of the frigate Mermaid, had promifed him to admit me on his quarter-deck, and defired me to wait on him with his compliments, and acquaint him that I was the young man he had mentioned. The Captain received me very gracioufly, and faid, the Mermaid would fail in a month to Newfoundland, and therefore the fooner I went on board her at Portfmouth, the better. I made all difpatch poffible with my little equipment for the voyage, and after having waited on Sir Charles to return him thanks, fet out for Portfmouth.

I continued two years on board this fhip; every fummer we went to Newfoundland, under the command of a Commodore, and returned by the end of November; but as nothing particular happened worth mentioning, I fhall shall pass over these two voyages, taking notice only that I was very civilly treated by the Captain and the inferior officers.

When I returned the second time, I had letters from home, acquainting me with the melancholy news of the death of my dear Mother, whom I very sincerely lamented, as she justly deserved. Though I was very happy on board the Mermaid, there was no variety in our voyages, and Sir Charles, when he knew my wish to change into another ship, very soon indulged me. I was rated midshipman on board the Fox, Captain Fortescue, going up the Mediterranean. Here I had an opportunity of seeing Marseilles, Barcelona, Genoa, Leghorn, and Naples. I continued on board her, till we came home in Autumn 1771. When we lay in Portsmouth harbour, I heard a vast deal

of

of Captain Cooke's voyage round the world in the Endeavour bark, accompanied by Meſſrs. Banks and Solander. The wonderful relations which were made concerning it, and the report of two ſhips fitting out to proceed in the Spring under the ſame commander on further diſcoveries, occaſioned in me an eager deſire to make one of the adventurers. I got leave in the winter for a month to ſee my friends; and when at home, could not be eaſy in my mind till I mentioned it to my Father, and aſked his leave to apply to Sir Charles to get me a birth in one of them. I found him very averſe to ſo long and unuſual a voyage, but finding me ſo much bent on it, he at laſt reluctantly complied. Had my dear Mother been alive, I believe ſhe never would have been prevailed on to give her conſent.

Sir

Sir Charles Saunders, when applied to, entered warmly into the affair, applauding my spirit; for none knew better than he, the dangers and fatigues of such a voyage. Through his interest I was again rated Midshipman on board the Adventure, Captain Furneaux, and was made infinitely happy; little foreseeing the many distresses and hardships which were in store for me.

Of this voyage I shall give but a very short abstract, and that only during the time I was on board the Adventure; leaving the reader to receive further information, from the well wrote and candid relation of it, given to the Public by Captain Cooke.

The Resolution and Adventure sailed from Plymouth Sound on the 13th of July 1772, and anchored in Funchiale road in the island of Madeira the

the 29th. Here we took on board a sufficient quantity of wine; and left it August 1st. Not having water enough to carry us to the Cape of Good Hope, Captain Cooke thought proper to put into Port Praya in the island of St. Jago on the 10th; where we stayed till the 14th; and, on the 30th of October, came to an anchor in Table Bay.

Here we took in bread, spirits, and other necessaries; and sailed from the Cape of Good Hope the 22d of November, in search of a southern continent. We now stood to high southern latitudes, where nothing was to be seen but islands of ice, and sea birds; the former, however, or rather the loose ice, supplied us with excellent fresh water, after the external part had drained off. In this manner, and as far south as the ice would give us leave,

leave, did we furround one half of the fouthern hemifphere without feeing any continent. We feparated from the Refolution in a gale of wind, on February 9th, 1773, and got into Queen Charlotte's Sound in New Zealand April the 10th, where the Refolution joined us May 18th. Both fhips had been 117 days without feeing land, and had failed 3660 leagues. Winter now beginning, we failed from New Zealand June 7th, and arrived at Otaheite Auguft 16th; where we were in great danger of running upon a reef of rocks, and the Advenventure loft three anchors irrecoverably, the Refolution being more fortunate.

At this, and the neighbouring iflands, we continued till September 17th, getting all the frefh provifions we poffibly could, wooding and watering.

tering. During this time Captain Furneaux took on board a native of Ulietea called Omai. From Ulietea we fteered to the Friendly Iflands, and arrived at that of Amfterdam October 3d. On the 7th, failed toward New Zealand, and on the 30th, were again feparated from the Refolution in a gale of wind. We were not able to fetch Queen Charlotte's Sound, but were obliged to anchor, November the 9th, in Tolaga Bay; and on the 30th, got at laft into Charlotte Sound in New Zealand. There Captain Furneaux found, by a letter Captain Cooke had left for him, in a corked bottle hid under ground, with directions to dig for it, that the Refolution had been there, and failed on the 24th. We immediately fet about getting the fhip ready for fea; and by the 17th of December fhe was fo.

That

That day Captain Furneaux sent Mr. Rowe and Mr. Woodhoufe, Midshipmen, with eight of his best hands, on shore, in the large cutter, to gather wild greens, such as cellery and scurvy-grafs, to carry to sea with us. I being a keen sportsman, begged leave to go with them, to try if I could meet with any game; which being granted, I took a fusee with me, and sufficient ammunition, both ball and small shot; with some baubles to trade with the natives, if I met with any. I know not by what mistake Captain Furneaux, in his letter to Captain Cooke, which he left for him at the Cape, makes no mention of my being in the cutter. It proved, however, a happy one; for tho' my family have been in the greatest anxiety about my fate, they had no apprehensions of my being devoured by creatures of my own species.

The

The cutter firſt went to Eaſt Bay; but what was wanted not being in plenty there, we proceeded to Grafs Cove, where there was abundance. While the men were employed in gathering them, I walked into the woods, to try if I could meet with any game; not having the leaſt ſuſpicion of an attack from the natives. My ſport happened to carry me farther from our men than I intended; and I was greatly alarmed with the report of ſome muſket ſhot from that quarter. I immediately ran full ſpeed to their aſſiſtance; but before I got half-way, the firing ceaſed; and a horrid ſcream was ſet up, which could only come from the ſavages; and ſeemed not of diſtreſs, but victory. This ſtopped my career, and made ſelf-preſervation appear a neceſſary

cessary duty. I therefore proceeded with caution towards the place; resolving, if possible, to keep myself unseen, by the covert of the woods, while I explored the scene of action. But, good God! what a horrid spectacle appeared! all our men lying dead on the place, and surrounded by some hundreds of savages, of both sexes and of all ages. I was at first tempted to fire among them; but considering that by so doing I should put them on searching for me, and it would be impossible to escape, I restrained my resentment; but continued sometime longer in my lurking-place, to observe their actions. But how shall I relate the horrid feast which was prepared for that multitude? the fire was kindled, and the mangled limbs of my poor countrymen and shipmates, were put on it to broil for their

their unnatural repaſt; nay even ſome parts I ſaw devoured. I could ſtand it no longer, horror ſeized me! my whole frame was in the moſt dreadful tremour! and ſcarcely able to ſupport me in withdrawing into the woods: I ſtaggered about without knowing what I did, or meant to do; excepting only the getting at a diſtance from thoſe vile cannibals.

By degrees as I effected that, my ſtrength and ſpirits gradually recovered themſelves; but ſtill in great agitation of mind, I preſſed forward with all my ſpeed, liſtening to the leaſt noiſe made by the wind among the trees; and often looking back to ſee if I was not purſued.

When I had got four or five miles from the fatal place, I began to conſider how my getting back to the Adventure

venture was to be effected. Having come from her by water, I had given little attention to the courfe of the country; and the hurry of fpirits I had been in, together with the thicknefs of the woods, made me utterly at a lofs which way to direct my fteps.

After reflecting for fome time on what courfe I was to take, while I refted myfelf a little; the neceffity of making an attempt to find her out, determined me to take the line of direction (for road or path there was none) which feemed moft probable to lead me to Charlotte Sound. This I did with lefs hurry and more compofure than before; but with a very heavy heart; confidering the danger I run from the favages, the uncertainty of finding the fhip, and the want of neceffary fubfiftence in that dreary defart. Having purfued this

this refolution for fome hours, and greatly fatigued, night came on; which called my attention, how it was to be paffed in greateft fafety from favage beafts (if any there were), or ftill more favage men. My deliberation was of fhort continuance; a tree prefented itfelf to my view with thick fpreading branches, which promifed at leaft to preferve me from the former. I climbed up into it, and feated myfelf as commodioufly as the nature of the place would admit; but fuch a dreary melancholy night, fure no mortal ever paffed. The fhocking fcene was always prefent to my imagination; nor could I help reflecting on myfelf for the foolifh ardour I had conceived for making this voyage; which was in fome meafure contrary to my Father's inclinations. Thefe and fimilar reflections hindered me from closing my eyes the whole night; and when day appeared, it brought me but small comfort. The necessity of my situation, however, roused me to new exertions for finding out the Adventure; and, by putting my confidence in an all-seeing Providence, my resolution was wonderfully supported.

My hunger this day became very craving; and tho' there were birds flying about in great numbers, I was afraid the report of my gun, or the lighting of a fire might discover me. I therefore contented myself with nuts, berries, wild celery, and fern roots, which I found in the woods; venturing rather to run the risk of their being unwholesome, than to incur the other more imminent danger. I had yesterday charged my piece with ball, and kept constantly

ſtantly on my guard, but was reſolved not to fire but on the utmoſt neceſſity of ſelf-defence; and happily during this whole day, tho' I ſaw ſome ſavages roaming about (probably in ſearch of game), yet I was not obſerved by them.

Notwithſtanding the unevenneſs of the ground, the thick underwood I had often to force my way through, and ſlender diet; by my computation I muſt that day have travelled ſeventeen or eighteen miles; and perhaps was not nearer the ſhip, than when I ſet out. Thus greatly fatigued, and very difconſolate, I again took up my lodgings for the night on a tree; but paſſed it more agreeably than the preceding one. For kind ſleep came to my relief, and for a time lulled my cares; but even that was not without alloy, for the ſame idea which, awake,

wake, affected me so much, was presented to me in my dreams. Much refreshed, I proceeded the third day on the same (as I feared) fruitless pursuit as before, keeping the line of direction I had hitherto followed, no reason appearing to me for altering it. My success that morning in procuring nourishment being very bad, about noon my hunger became intolerable; and to such a degree violent, that it even got the better of my fear of the savages. I was besides tempted with the sight of birds flying round me, without being alarmed at the human form; and was on the brink of a pure running stream to allay my thirst. I could resist no longer, but drawing the ball, charged with small shot, and let drive amongst them; three fell dead on the

the ground, which were a kind of wood pigeons. My piece was immediately charged again with ball; and then I kindled a fire with some dry leaves and bits of sticks; my birds were soon pulled, gutted and broiled. It was happy for me that I had loaded again, for scarcely had I voraciously devoured two of them, when I perceived two of the natives coming fiercely upon me with spears in their hands (being led to seek me out by the report of the gun, or the sight of the fire). I own that horror seized me at the sight of them, and scarcely doubting of sharing the fate of my ship-mates, I got presently on my legs, and cocked my piece; my courage recovered itself somewhat, and I stood ready to receive them. When they got within twenty yards of me I fired, and brought one of

them to the ground; had the other rufhed in upon me before I could charge, I was undone; but he immediately fled, which eafed me of my fears. I alfo quitted the place in no fmall trepidation from the narrow efcape I had made. When I had got to fome diftance from the place, and had in a great meafure recovered myfelf; the neceffity into which I had been brought of killing a human creature, gave me a good deal of concern. But when I confidered that by all laws, human and divine, felf-defence is allowed of; my mind was perfectly at eafe on that fcore. This train of thought led me to confider, the wide difference there is, in the manners and ways of thinking of different human beings. In nothing more remarkable than what I had beheld thefe favages guilty of, the
devouring

devouring their own fpecies; which all civilized nations hold in the utmoft dēteftation; and even believe it an innate principle in our natures. I then concluded with myfelf, as that was not one, there was no fuch thing; but education and habit was all in all; and had I been born in that part of New Zealand, I moft certainly fhould have been a cannibal. This ferved, in fome meafure, to foften my refentment againft thefe poor favages, tho' I was firmly refolved to keep out of their hands.

Having neither feen nor heard any fierce animals, but only fuch timid ones as a fpecies of deer, hares and foxes; I ventured to lie this night on a dry fpot of ground, well covered with withered grafs, which I pulled and made a bed of, under a tree;

a tree; which was quite luxury to what I had been ufed to.

To give a minute and uninterefting journal of my peregrinations, and fubfiftence in the woods, in fearch of the Adventure, would be full of repetitions, and tirefome to the reader: I fhall only therefore fay in general, that after feveral times changing my courfe, at laft, on the 23d of December, I found myfelf on the fide of Charlotte Sound, where fhe lay; which I knew by certain marks; but to my great mortification, found her there no longer. I got up on the higheft ground near the fea, to look out for her; and faw her under fail about a league off; fhe having only failed that morning, as the wind was fair and a frefh breeze; fo that if I had come

but

but an hour fooner, I fhould have got on board. My fear of the favages did not now prevent my firing, and hanging out my handkerchief, faftened to the end of a long ftick, by way of fignal to the people on board the Adventure; but they had not obferved it, as they kept on their way, and were foon at a great diftance.

The hope of being able to join the Adventure, had hitherto fupported my fpirits; but when I faw her irretrievably gone, my heart funk into the moft abject defpondency. I fat motionlefs as a ftatue, eyeing her as fhe went from me, and death feemed, then, the moft defirable event that could befall me. While in this fituation of mind and body, I was alarmed with the hollowing of the natives at fome diftance

tance from me. I ſtarted up in a manner mechanically, to view whereabouts they were, and how I ſhould make my eſcape from them; for though death would have been deſirable, the being eat by men ſhocked my nature, and I could not bear the thoughts of it. Fortunately they were not very near, and I had ſufficient time to make my eſcape from them, on the contrary direction to that from whence their voices came. Some philoſophical reader will perhaps cry out here; What was it to you, what became of your body after your death, whether it was eat by worms or ſavages? I grant it; but when a ſtrong impreſſion is made on the imagination, a man cannot think philoſophically. And I queſtion whether ever a philoſopher of them all, in my ſituation, would not have

have endeavoured to preferve his earthly part from the jaws of the cannibals.

But to return to my travels. This alarm roufed me from my languid defpondency; and I refolved, with the affiftance of a good providence, to ftruggle againft all difficulties with fortitude; leaving the event to the all-difpofing will of the creator and preferver of all mankind.

As I had now no farther bufinefs in that part of the country, and knew from charts, that New Zealand (as it is called by the Europeans) is a great extent of country, divided into iflands, lying contiguous to each other, and feparated by narrow feas; I therefore refolved to explore fome other part of it, where perhaps men of more humanity might be found,

than

than thofe I fo much feared and detefted. I therefore turned my face weftward, and marched on with a good deal of fpirit, but with great caution. The hufbanding my amunition became now a matter of great concern, as I had not a great deal, and no poffibility of a fupply, but by what would make it unneceffary. I refolved therefore never to fire, but upon an abfolute neceffity, either in felf-defence, or when fubfiftence could not otherwife be procured; and when I did, not to wafte my fhot on fmall birds, but always fire at large ones, deer or hares, that would fubfift me feveral days.

As I had got near the fea, it appeared moft eligible to keep hold of the coaft; but ftill a little way within the fkirts of the woods. Five or
fix

six days paffed, without any thing happening which was material; at the end of that time, the coaft turned a little to the left hand, as if it was going to form a Bay; and in three days more, I could fee land on the other fide, but at a great diftance. As I proceeded on, the land ftill appeared nearer; until at laft it feemed not to be above four or five leagues over, at the place I then was, but widened again farther on. I concluded that to be therefore the narroweft part of that channel.

As mortals know the prefent danger and difagreeablenefs of their fituations, but what will happen by a change is wifely kept from them, they are always ready to grafp at any opportunity of freeing themfelves, from the burdens with whofe weight

weight they are oppreſſed. This was my caſe, I looked on the oppoſite ſhore with deſiring eyes, and hoped that if I could be conveyed thither, more hoſpitable people might be met with, whoſe friendly intercourſe would make my life paſs more agreeably; for the ſolitary ſtate I was in was become almoſt inſupportable.

The great inclination I had, to find ſome means of paſſing that ſtrait, kept me near it; and ſet me on contriving how it might be effected; but as I had no better inſtruments than a knife and hanger to cut down trees, or faſhion them afterwards into a raft or canoe, the thing appeared impoſſible, or would at leaſt be the labour of months. And how that could be carried on for ſo long a time, without being diſcovered, was not eaſy to conceive.

I met

I met here with a delicacy, of which I had been always very fond; it was very fine oyfters; there happened to be a bed of them near the fhore, to which I had frequent recourfe. One day, as I was going to vifit my hoard, as I thought it, a canoe with one of the natives in it, ftruck my eye-fight, and greatly furprifed me. My caution had become fo habitual, that I drew back, mechanically, out of his fight, and then confidered ferioufly, on what was to be done. Providence feemed to have provided this canoe for my efcape, as there was almoft a certainty of fhooting the owner, by my taking aim coolly from a reft. The morality however of this action did not feem quite blamelefs, notwithftanding my unfortunate fituation; murder

der and robbery appeared to me great crimes; and probably too, of a man who had no concern in the deftruction of my countrymen. I rejected the idea, without being much tempted to do otherwife; refolving only to watch his motions, and obferve to what place he carried it. He loaded it with oyfters, and afterwards paddled it two or three miles along the coaft, where feveral women met him; he then unloaded the canoe, and they carried the oyfters away in bafkets, very handfomely made. When that was done, he paddled it back again, and hid it in a fmall creek, not far from the oyfter bank; which was very thick of under-wood, and departed. Though I fcrupled fhooting the favage, and robbing him of his canoe; the borrowing of it to crofs the

the strait, did not, in my circumstances, appear so inexcusable; as it was possible he might recover it again, some time or other. The danger, however, of going four or five leagues, in so poor a vessel, deserved to be maturely weighed; especially as the waves might be very much agitated, in so broad a channel, if it should happen to blow any wind. This was soon over-ruled, the danger of being drowned, and made a feast for fishes, had little horror in it, when opposed to the risk I every day was exposed to. As the continuance of my voyage might be long, considering I had no sail; it was necessary to provide sea-stores: for which half a deer was dressed; and, together with fern roots and plenty of oysters, made up my stock. My greateſt difficulty was about freſh water, having no veſſel to hold any. This difficulty ſeemed inſurmountable; but as I was reſolved on the attempt, ſome ſhift muſt be made: no other occurred, after long thinking on the ſubject, but to *fill my hat* as full as it could hold; taking care to drink plentifully before I ſet out, that a longer time might elapſe before my precious element was begun upon.

Thus victualled, I ſet out one fine morning on my voyage, when the wind was moderate, and with an ebb tide. Paddling, was what I had not been accuſtomed to, and therefore was awkward at; but a willing mind goes a great way in learning to paddle, as well as in every thing elſe. While the ebb continued,

nued, the water was smooth, and I made my way through it pretty fast; but about noon when it began to flow, there was a considerable agitation, and topling, owing to the narrowness of the channel; which made my labour much more difficult and fatiguing. I strained every nerve however to get on, though apparently much flower than before. Luckily for me, it proved a fine night; part of which was passed in resting myself, and taking some refreshment. In the morning I found myself half-way over; but the much desired country, had a very unpromising appearance; exhibiting bleak mountains covered over with heath, excepting near the shore, and scarcely a tree to be seen.

 I now observed, that since the mid channel was passed, the flood carried me me towards the fhore, and the ebb on the contrary from it. To fave my labour then, I refted myfelf during the former, and paddled ftoutly during the latter, to prevent my lofing the ground I had got. In the afternoon, it became fqually with rain; the laft was very agreeable, though it wet me to the fkin, as it recruited my flock of water; but the fqualls of wind put me often in great danger of overfetting. Though I' had got within half a league of the fhore, when night came on, furely never was one paffed more difagreeably. It was extremely dark, and the wind increafed to a ftorm; fo that I expected every moment to be overfet, or dafhed againft the rocks. Towards morning it abated, and when day appeared, I found myfelf within

half

half a mile of a fandy beach: my whole force was exerted to reach it, and with fuccefs; for which I fell on my knees, and returned thanks to the all-powerful maker and governour of the world.

CHAP. II.

The miserable condition of the Author in Taupiniera. An account of that extraordinary People.

THE firſt thing I did, after getting on ſhore, was to take a view of the country, I had ſo anxiouſly longed to be an inhabitant of. But great was my diſappointment! bleak and barren mountains only preſented themſelves to my ſight. No houſes for inhabitants of any kind, and only ſome ſtunted trees, here and there in the hollows, which afforded no ſhelter from either ſun or rain. I roamed about with a heavy heart, as there ſeemed no poſſibility of ſubſiſting, and was almoſt tempted to return

return in the canoe to the oppofite fhore: but that idea kept not its ground long; my deteftation of it foon recurred to my imagination. But, befides, as all my provifions were expended, how could fuch a paffage be undertaken without more, and where were they to be found? In this difconfolate ftate of mind, I wandered about, without any object in view; when happily a clear ftream of excellent water prefented itfelf. This gave me fome confolation, and I drank freely of it. It then occurred to me, that though the land feemed to produce nothing for the fupport of human life, yet the fea might: recollecting the excellent oyfters on the oppofite fhore. I examined then the beach carefully for fhell-fifh of any fort, but for fome time

time with little fuccefs; at laft cockles, mufcles, and fome other kinds with which I was unacquainted, were found in great plenty; and with them my hunger was allayed. While 1 was bufy in fulfilling the moft neceffary of all duties, the prefervation of the individual, I happened accidentally to caft my eyes on the fand, and was much furprifed to obferve great numbers of prints of human feet. This gave me inconceivable joy; but where thefe people dwelt, as no houfes were to be feen, puzzled me greatly. It was plain to me, that many hours had not paffed fince they had been there, becaufe the flood tide coming in, would have effaced the impreffions. I then compared the fize of their feet with my own, by making prints in the fand

clofe

close by theirs, and found mine at least two inches longer. This made me conclude, that only children had been there; but where should they come from? The affair seemed inexplicable, and I resolved to keep thereabout 'till it was cleared up: but where else could I go, with any certainty of subsisting?

My thoughts were next employed, about the means of passing the night, in some sort of comfort and safety: to which end I pitched upon a spot, above high-water mark, betwixt two rocks; leaving just room for my bed, which I intended making of the heath which grew upon the mountains. Climbing up then the nearest, I pulled a sufficient quantity for my intention; but, upon examining the shrub with attention, it seemed of a different

species

species from what we have in England, though for my purpose preferable, being softer, and of a more agreeable smell. When night came on, I lay down upon it; hoping (notwithstanding many anxious thoughts about my situation) that sleep would for a time, release me from my cares; more especially, as the two preceding nights had scarcely afforded me any rest. About an hour after, when it was, as I judged, low water, a noise something betwixt the human voice, and grunt of a hog disturbed me. I immediately started up, when there appeared (though the night was dark) about a dozen of human creatures of a low size, catching shell-fish on the beach. Their small size made me imagine they were children, as I had before done,

done, from the impreffion of their feet on the fand; I therefore went boldly up to them, and in the Otaheite language afked them where they lived. In place of any anfwer to my queftion, they ran away full fpeed: I followed them, and called with a tone of authority to ftop; but it only increafed their hafte to get from me. Both my curiofity and intereft were fo much concerned, to know who they were, that I refolved to try if the report of my fufee, would intimidate them enough to ftop their flight. I fired it up in the air, upon which they all fell down, and lay without motion, thinking no doubt they were killed. Going up to them, I faid kindly, and without any figns of anger, that they were in no danger

*

from

from me, as I wanted their affiftance both in food and lodging. The
poor creatures then recovered themfelves a little; and upon their knees,
holding up both their hands, feemed
to implore my mercy. I fpoke again
to them in the fame mild manner,
that they need fear nothing, but there
was no appearance of their underftanding me. Seeing that I had only
figns left, by which they might be
made to underftand me, I tried to
make them comprehend, by different
geftures, that they fhould return to
their former occupations, and with
much difficulty fucceeded; whilft I
carefully obferved them, as well as
the darknefs of the night would permit. My firft difcovery was, that
they were not children, but full
grown perfons of a thick, fquat
make

make, and only about four foot and a half high. Some young ones there alſo were; and all were buſy in gathering ſhell-fiſh, and carrying them without high-water mark; where they laid them in ſeparate heaps, as if belonging to different families. My next obſervation was, that they ſeemed to go about their buſineſs, with as much eaſe and regularity, as if it was broad day-light. But I was ſtill more ſurpriſed, when many of them threw themſelves into the water; and ſwimming for a little while, dived, bringing always up with them one or two fiſh. Theſe things I could not comprehend, but concluded it was owing to habit, which produces ſurpriſing effects. What next came into my thoughts, was, why theſe people had not come

alſo

alſo at the former ebb tide in the day-time; but that was ſoon accounted for, by the fear they might be in of the cannibals from the oppoſite ſhore; and ſeemed a convincing reaſon to me, that I ought to be upon my guard, againſt their attacks even there.

When the ebb was ſpent, and the flood coming in, the natives having finiſhed for the preſent, all came to me, and made an offer of what they had got in rude baſkets, which I declined. One of the men then made me underſtand by ſigns, that he intreated me to go home with him. This invitation was accepted, as I was curious to ſee their habitations. We ſet out for his abode about two hours before day, attended by another grown perſon (probably a female) and a child, and walked but a quar-

ter of a mile, before we entered a cave of a pretty large fize, dug in the fide of the mountain. It had a narrow entrance of eight or ten feet long, and then grew much wider in a roundifh form; this I learned from my feeling, for it was much darker in it than in the open air. The roof was fo low, that I was obliged to ftand almoft double; and my fenfe of fmelling was more offended than it could have been in any pig-ftye in England. All this my curiofity made me bear for fome time, in hopes fome kind of light would be produced: but as I heard by the motion of their jaws, they had begun to eat their fifh raw, and felt fome preffed againft my hands, hearing at the fame time an articulate grunt of invitation. (as I fuppofed), I could ftand it no longer,
but

but groped my way out again; and happy I thought myfelf when refreſhed by the open air. One of them followed me, and faid fomething, which I fuppofed was preffing me to return, but was civilly excufed by me. I took as good notice of the fituation of the cave, as the darknefs would permit, and made the beſt of my way to the heath bed, where I ſleeped comfortably till noon.

When ſleep left me, my cares returned; and my thoughts were for fome time employed on the difappointment of my hopes, in meeting with a fociable people on this coaſt. For what fociety could I have with fuch ſtupid, and nafty animals? whofe language, feemed to differ little, from the fimple and uniform founds, with which nature has endued many brutes;

brutes; and whofe habitations were not to be endured by a human creature, bred in decency and cleanlinefs. The only thing with refpect to them which was favourable, was, that they did not feem fierce or dangerous, and had conceived a great refpect for me; which I might improve to my advantage. When I arofe, and walked on the beach, it was quite as folitary as the day before, though it was then ebb tide, not the leaft appearance of a human creature. This was accounted for by me, in the fame manner as the night before; from the fear of irruptions of the cannibals from the oppofite coaft; and I concluded it neceffary to be in more fecurity from them, than where my bed at prefent was placed. After mature deliberation,

tion, I could fall on no better contrivance, than imitating the natives; either in finding an uninhabited cave, which I might get cleaned out, or fetting them to work to dig me a new one, if I obferved by day-light, that thofe in ufe were not damp or unwholefome. Having come to this refolution, after fatisfying my hunger with fome fhell-fifh, and my thirft at the limpid ftream, I fet out in queft of my hoft's habitation, and after no very long fearch luckily found it.

I entered without ceremony, and having got to the bottom of the cave, which was nearly as dark as the night before; I found the three inhabitants faft afleep, lying on the bare ground, fnorting and fnoring, in the midft of putrid fifh, and their own nafti- nefs,

nefs, which different naufeous fmells had almoft overcome me. My hafte to be gone, made me fhake and roufe one of the full grown perfons, with very little ceremony, and I at laft fucceeded in waking him, for it happened to be a male. I made him get up, and taking his hand, in a manner forced him out of the cave. When he was in the light, what firft drew my attention, was his face; which, though of the human form, had fome refemblance to a hog; like caricature drawings I had feen. He had a thick bufhy beard, and (dirt excepted) was as naked as when he came into the world. No tattoings, nor ear or nofe ornaments, thefe people being too fluggifh, to have any vanity of that fort. After having fatisfied my curiofity, with regard to his form,

E 3   I made

I made figns to him, that I wanted a cave to fleep in; but he took not the leaft notice of them, either by word or gefture; nor had frequent repetitions of thofe and others, any more effect upon him. Sufpecting then that he was ftill afleep, I fpoke loud, but not in a threatening tone: this affected him, and convinced me he was awake. After this I tried all the means I could think of, to make him go along with me, but without fuccefs. This appearing the effects of fulkinefs, I took him by the hand and forced him on; but though he followed me, it was like a blind man who depends entirely on his guide. Being much furprifed at this phenomenon, I examined his eyes; and to my great furprife, found they refembled thofe of a mole, more than of a hu-

Inld. Bowman del: et Sculpt.   See Page 54

I m:
cav(
leaf
or
titi(
effe
tha
bu(
affe
wa
me
go
ce{
ful
an
fol
wl
Be
m(
m
bl

a human creature. This discovery seemed to account for the blindness of these people in a full light, and their clear-sightedness in the dark; but it was so much out of the common course of nature, that I knew not how to credit it, and therefore left it for further examination. As this man could be of no assistance to me, I led him back to his cave, and laid him down in his stye.

Seeing my dependance (at least in the day-time) must be upon myself, I began to examine the nature of the cave; and found it was dug out of a soft rock, was very dry, and consequently wholesome. My next endeavours were used, towards finding an empty one, which might be appropriated to my own use; but as they were few in number, all that I could fee, were inhabited, and all as nafty as the firft. After almoft defpairing of fuccefs, I faw, at fome diftance, the mouth of one not yet examined: it proved to be only half made, and for fome reafon or other never completed, but was perfectly fweet and clean. This charmed me, and was the more agreeable, as it was not fo deep, but that the external air would breathe upon me, to whofe open expofure I had been fo long accuftomed. My bed of heath was my next care, which was eafily removed to my new habitation; and as no other fewel could be got to drefs the fifh, (which I had no doubt the natives would fupply me with) but the fame heath: I pulled a fufficient quantity of it, and laid it in my cave; refolving that night, to treat the natives with a feaft a feaft of their own catching, while I at the fame time made an experiment on their organs of fight.

At the ufual time I went to the beach, where a much greater number of the natives were affembled, than the night before; there were near forty perfons, of all ages, and of both fexes; probably from the report which had been fpread of my wonderful appearance.

As foon as they faw me approaching, they all came and made their fubmiffions on their knees, and with uplifted hands; which I moft gracioufly received, and then made figns to them to go on with their fifhing. Every thing paffed in the fame manner as the night before, and they catched a great many fifh, of different kinds and fizes, but all unknown to me;

me; which however I found afterwards were all wholefome and well tafted. I was now thoroughly convinced, that the fight of thefe people was fo good in the dark, that they faw the fifh lying afleep at the bottom of the water, and confequently had little difficulty in feizing them, when they dived.

When all was over, they came to me as before, and made an offer of what they had caught: I took a little from each family, and made figns for them all to follow me; which was immediately complied with. The fcene was at the front of my cave. My firft operation was gutting the fifh with my knife; which feemed new to them, as it occafioned much grunting in the circle around me. I then lighted a fire, and made a confiderable

ble blaze, to fee what effect it would have on their fight; and, as I expected, they seemed all ftruck blind immediately; running from it in great confufion, and tumbling one over another. As foon as the blaze was over, they came around me again, when putting the fifh on the embers 'till they were fufficiently done, I began to eat them, and offered fome to every one; but few accepted, and fewer, after tafting, feemed to approve my cookery; fo powerful is cuftom, however contrary to reafon and nature it may be. As foon as the repaft was over, I difmiffed my guefts with great kindnefs; who no doubt wondered very much at what they had feen, and could not take me for any thing lefs than a divinity.

I was now fettled in the neighbourhood of thefe wretched creatures;
and

and though there feemed nothing to be feared from their malevolence or treachery; yet, excepting the fifh they gave me to fuftain a miferable life, as to any fociety, I had better have had as many dogs or horfes for my companions; much more cleanly, and very near as fenfible, animals. Thofe would have been near me whenever I chofe; but I was obliged to imitate thefe, in my hours of reft as well as in my habitation; for in the daytime all was folitary and difmal, nor was there a poffibility of any intercourfe with them in their vile habitations.

Being refolved however to make the moft of my fituation, I cultivated a kind of intimacy with the natives at the beach, and before my cave; the better to examine into their bodily peculiarities, and mental faculties.

ties. For that purpose I endeavoured to learn the language, which seemed to be no very difficult matter, being a very simple one; and how could it be otherwise with people who necessarily must have so few ideas. The poor creatures were willing to oblige me, as far as their capacities would permit; and when they once understood, that by pointing to any particular part of the body or thing, I meant they should name it in their language, they immediately complied. By this common and simple method we made some progress, for I also named it to them in English.

In the course of my schooling with different masters, I learnt that they had no word for fire; they always shaking their heads whenever I pointed to it; which was a convincing proof to me, that they were entirely ignorant

rant of it before. Their blindnefs in the day, and clear-fightednefs in the dark, became from repeated obfervations a fact not to be doubted by me; however contrary it may be to the common courfe of nature all over the world, both in men and moft kinds of animals. I fhall not pretend to account for this phenomenon, unlefs the refemblance of their eyes to thofe of moles, may be thought fufficient for that purpofe. But it may be afked, Did nature form thefe people's eyes, on purpofe for their peculiar way of living in the fide of that mountain? To that I fhall not pretend to give an anfwer, but leave it to naturalifts to difcufs. I have been told by a learned Phyfician fince my return, to whom I had given an account of thefe extraordinary mortals,

that

that there is a diforder in the eyes (but a very rare one) called nyɑ̃ta lopia, which exactly refembles the fight of this fpecies of people. But it is not to be imagined, that a whole people (tho' far from numerous) can be equally difeafed in that manner. It was a confiderable time before I could find out, whether thefe people had any name they diftinguifhed themfelves by; and at laft I learned that they called themfelves Taupinierans; but to write it in the manner it is pronounced by them, would far exceed my power, and I fhall therefore leave it to the imagination of the reader.

Having ftill fome anxiety about a vifit from the cannibals of the oppofite coaft, I one night carried feveral of my friends to the place where the canoe

canoe lay, letting them know that I had come in it from the oppofite coaft. This feemed another novelty to them, and they had no name for it; which gave me no fmall fatisfaction, as I might now fleep in quiet, without fearing fuch difagreeable guefts. It had lain a little on my confcience, that I had not been able to return that canoe; but as there was no poffibility of doing it, I was obliged to leave the reftoration of it to fortune.

The only Taupinieran whom I fuffered to enter my habitation, was a boy of five or fix years old from the next cave to me. All animals when young, are prettier, and more playful, than thofe come to maturity; this child diverted me, and had taken a particular fancy to my company.

pany. He sometimes stole to my cave in the dusk of the evening, (which was their morning) before it was quite dark, when we used to play together. One evening when we were at romps, I discovered to my great surprise, that he had a short tail, like that of a young pig; being scarcely able to believe my own feeling, I examined it over and over, and found it an undoubted truth. Though I had no doubt of finding the whole race formed in the same manner, it would have been inexcusable in me, to have neglected ascertaining the fact incontestably; especially when it might be done with so little trouble: the result was, that both sexes were furnished with these small appendages. I am apprehensive that my veracity may be here liable to suspicion;

fufpicion ; which has fet me on reading books of travels, and examining the opinions of authors on that fubject, fince my return home. Great was my joy, to find that feveral travellers had feen men with fuch rear appendixes; which a learned judge in the northern part of this ifland has made a collection of, and, after a thorough examination, gives entire credit to. It is alfo very fatisfactory to me, that this my account of the Taupinierans, will give a fingular pleafure to this learned gentleman ; who has been fneered at by fome fmatterers in knowledge, on this very account.

The females were no ways diftinguifhed from the males in their drefs ; the love of fhow fuppofed to be innate in that fex, took not place here; perhaps

perhaps from a want of the poffibility of gratifying it. But I muft do thefe ladies the juftice to declare, that on feeing fome glafs beads, which all favages are fond of, they took no pleafure in them, and declined their acceptance. By the advances which feveral of them made me, they however feemed to have no objection to a tender connection; but I gave none of them any encouragement, as it was always my opinion, that wronging another in his bed was a very great crime. It may be perhaps faid, that my virtue was put under no great temptation. I grant it; but confidering my youth, health, and long abfence from Otaheite, many in my circumftances might not have withftood it.

Marriage amongft thefe people is contracted with little ceremony, there being

being neither prieft nor magiftrate; and is as eafily diffolved, both being dependent on the will of the parties.

Paternal government in each family, is the only one known; all being alike in authority; and if any difpute happens about their fifh, it is referred to their male neighbours, whofe verdict is always decifive. I could not learn that they had any religion, except a kind of veneration for the moon; which they pay when firft feen after the change, by falling down on their faces for fome moments. It did not appear to me to be on account of the light fhe gave, as that they would willingly be excufed from; but becaufe it was the fineft fight, which came within their fphere of vifion; for they have not the leaft idea of the fun.

The

The number of that fingular fpecies of men at this place, was under fifty; but whether there were any at other beaches on the coaft I could not learn. They are fo furrounded with mountains, that thefe people have no communication with them, if there are.

I had now lived about fix weeks with thefe wretched mortals, and had learned a great many words of their language. It may be eafily imagined, that I did not pafs my time fo agreeably among them, as not to frequently turn in my thoughts how to get out of their country. But great difficulties attended every refolution I could take. The idea of returning to the land from whence I came, could never get the leaft entrance; there was then no other alternative, but to crofs the mountains, or coaft along in the canoe, till some flat country appeared, which might promise inhabitants, and a supply of provisions. The simple inhabitants could give me no information with respect to either. If I crossed the mountains, being entirely ignorant of their extent, what danger might I run for want of provisions and water? and if on the other hand, my determination was for the coasting voyage, equal danger of the above wants presented themselves; especially as I had observed in coming over the strait, that the coast on each hand continued mountainous as far as I could see. The chance of meeting with barbarous inhabitants, I thought was equal either way, and must be risked.

At last I came to a resolution of crossing the mountains; and
could

could think of no other proviſions to carry with me, but fiſh dried in the ſun, which I immediately ſet about preparing. My walks for ſome days before I ſet out, were up different parts of the mountains, to reconnoitre the propereſt courſe to be taken. When my friends were informed of my reſolution, they ſhewed as much concern for loſing me, as their ſluggiſh diſpoſitions were capable of; and when I took leave of them, almoſt the whole ſhed tears, and wiſhed me ſuccefs.

I ſet out then on this arduous undertaking on the 28th of February, 1774, and recommending myſelf to the protection of a kind providence, began ſlowly to aſcend the mountain; knowing that the way to hold out long in any undertaking, was to purſue purfue it with fteadinefs and moderation; the weather was fine, and my fpirits good. For three hours I laboured up the firft mountain, and after taking breath a little, and viewing the ftill higher ones before me, began to defcend, and continued fo doing for two hours more. At the bottom of this vale appeared a ftream of running water, which tempted me to ftop there to recruit my ftrength with reft, and fuch refrefhment as my fifh and the ftream afforded. Here I loaded my piece with fmall fhot, believing there was nothing to fear from enemies of any kind; and that I might poffibly meet with growfe or fome other game, which would be a great regale.

I now purfued my journey, and laboured up a higher mountain than the

the former, but without feeing either bird or beaſt; at the top there was a fenſible alteration in the air, which was become much colder, tho' the wind had not changed. I could here fee before me mountains piled on mountains, and the hoary heads of the higheſt, covered with eternal ſnow, which almoſt ſtaggered my reſolution.

But taking courage, I defcended to another vale of fmall depth, for an hour brought me to its bottom; here I again found water, and being very much fatigued, refolved to take up my quarters there for the night. Heath for my bed, was found in plenty, the fame was my covering, and kept me tolerably warm in thofe bleak regions; fatigue lulled me to balmy reſt, where I flept as foundly, as in the beft chamber in England on a bed of down. Next morning much refrefhed, I renewed my labours, which feemed to have no end; and the cold began to be very intenfe. This day I had the luck to fhoot a brace of growfe, which made my dinner; and delicious morfels they were. I fortunately found a lake of frefh water on the very fummit of a mountain, or I fhould have been entirely deftitute; for the higher the mountains, the vales became more and more fhallow. The fecond night was paffed more difagreeably than the former, owing to the cold; nor could I make myfelf comfortable, with all the heath I fpread on me and around my bed.

I now approached the fnowy region, and was not without apprehenfions

henfions from the danger of paffing it; but confidering with myfelf that this danger overcome, the worſt would certainly be paſt, and I ſhould begin to defcend on the other fide; my refolution was ſtrengthened, and I advanced boldly to the undertaking. The fnow was hard enough to bear my weight, and for fome time I made a confiderable progrefs towards the fummit; the walking brifkly keeping me warm: but to my great grief, a ſhower of fnow came on, at firſt gently and in fmall drops; but afterwards in large flakes and attended with wind. While the fnow fhower continued moderate, I puſhed on, and believed myfelf at the very top of the mountain; but when it became heavy, the air was fo filled with it, and the atmofphere fo cloudy,

that

that I durst not venture to stir a step farther, for fear of losing my way, or tumbling down some precipice. Keeping then nearly in the same spot, I walked backwards and forwards to keep myself warm, but with very melancholy reflections; for should it continue till night, my fate was inevitable. In about an hour and a half however, it gave over snowing to my great joy; the sky cleared up, and I was entertained with the sight (tho' at a considerable distance), of a country well wooded and watered, which promised better days. I got clear of the snowy part of the mountain on the opposite side before night, and took up my quarters in the best manner I could. Game was more plentiful on this side, than the other; for besides the species of growse I had killed

killed before; there were some black cocks, and a few hares. The cold decreased as I got nearer the flat country, and in two days I reached it, to my great satisfaction.

CHAP.

CHAP. III.

Arrives in Olfactaria. Is adopted by that nation. Marries. Irruption of the Carnovirrians. Conclusion of that war. The Author elected a chief of the 3d, 2d, and 1st, orders. His ammunition exhausted, and he in fear of being degraded, from his want of practice with their weapons, as well as of a nose; gets the command of a large canoe, going to Auditante to exchange their skins. Arrives at Seripante.

BEFORE my descent into the flat country, I had loaded my fusee with ball, but with a resolution of not using it but on the utmost necessity; intending to run all risks for the mending of my condition; as my way of life for some time past was become

become intolerably irkfome. The defign I formed, was to apply to the firft human creature, I met with, in an open fearlefs manner as if in a civilifed country, to tell them my fituation, and defire their friendfhip. I hoped the Otaheite language which I had acquired in a tolerable degree, both by converfing with the natives of that and the other iflands when there, and with Omai, on board the Adventure, would enable me to put it in execution; as many of the natives of New Zealand underftood it, from the affinity it had with their own.

I entered then boldly into the woods, and looked out for their habitations. It was not long before a village (as it may be called) appeared; confifting of ten or twelve huts.

Going

Going into one of the largeſt of them, I found four of the natives lying on the ground, who ſeemed ſurpriſed at ſeeing me. I ſpoke to them in the Otaheite language with ſeeming unconcern, that I had belonged to a large canoe, which came from the fartheſt part of the world, and by a misfortune which happened to a ſmaller one on that coaſt, had been left behind. The oldeſt of the men anſwered me in their own language (which I underſtood) that I was welcome, and might depend on the friendſhip of the Olfactarian nation. He then invited me to lie down by them, and ſaid, we have ſeen men like you in a large canoe on this coaſt many moons ago; they were our good friends, and traded honeſtly with us. His deſcription anſwered ſo
exactly

exactly with the Endeavour that I affured him they were my countrymen; and he that commanded the large canoe then, had been lately on the coaft with two much larger ones; in one of which I had been. I now recollected that I had fome beads, nails, and other trade in my pockets, and taking them out, made an offer of fome to each of the Olfactarians, (as they called themfelves) beginning with the eldeft who had converfed with me. They all received my prefents with feeming pleafure, but efpecially the nails. I was now afked if I was hungry, and chofe to eat; and having anfwered in the affirmative, a young man was defired to call one of the women, to bring me fome venifon and fet it before me, which fhe did, in a more decent manner

manner than I expected. My appetite was good, which no doubt helped me to relish the food; for I never remember to have eat any thing with so much pleasure. After that, the same elderly man (whose name I afterwards learned was Uncomia, and one of their chiefs) said, that I had mentioned a misfortune, which had happened to a small canoe, desiring to know what it was. Upon this I gave him a circumstantial account of the whole affair, and of what had happened to me since, describing as well as I could Charlotte Sound, where the Adventure lay. When I had done speaking, he said, the nation who had used us so cruelly, was the Carnovirrians, who were their mortal enemies, and if I stayed long with them, I might have

an

an opportunity of being revenged. I anfwered him, that the religion profeffed in my country, forbid the revenging of injuries; but feeing he did not approve fuch tenets, I added with fpirit, But did not forbid us affifting our friends in a juft war; and that therefore he might depend on me, to the laft drop of my blood. This had the effect I defired; and he faid, Young man your behaviour pleafes me; you are at a vaft diftance from your own country, and perhaps may never have an opportunity of returning to it; I have fome influence with the Olfactarians, and if you have no objection, will propofe your adoption among us; when I fhall always look upon you with the fame affection, as I do on Ulopeia there prefent, who I defire you will embrace and love.

After having embraced his fon, I told him his offer was fo friendly, that provided I might think as I pleafed in religious matters, and be excufed from ornamenting my face in their manner, I warmly embraced it, and fhould always look on him as a father. In thefe indifferent points, he faid, he durft venture to fay the nation would difpenfe with me. This was not a refolution of mine taken up on the fudden, without having been thought of before, in cafe fuch a propofal fhould be made to me. In my circumftances what could I do better? It gave me fome weight with the people I was to live with; and my refufal might have had difagreeable confequences. I lay at his houfe, and next day he introduced me to all the warriors of the village, who received

received me gracioufly, and promifed to promote my adoption. In a week after, an affembly of the nation was held, when I was unanimoufly admitted an Olfactarian, by the name of Bowmania, with the abovementioned refervations. I was now dreffed like my new countrymen, which, to fay the truth, was very convenient for me; my fhoes being in very bad condition, my fingle fhirt almoft rotten on my back; and the reft of my clothes, with lying fo long rough, almoft quite wore out.

Some of my readers will no doubt wonder, that no notice is yet taken of my fufee, by thefe favages, or at leaft not mentioned by me; but he will be pleafed to recollect, that they were not quite ftrangers to fire-arms. They had now however an oppor-

tunity of examining one, more narrowly than ever they had before; and I gave them all the intelligence concerning every part of it, that I could. As favages who live upon hunting and fifhing, fubfift in a manner from hand to mouth; it was foon neceffary for them to recruit their flock of provifions; and as I propofed accompanying them, they defired that my fufee might be my only weapon, as they wanted to fee what advantage it had over theirs. This I readily complied with for this once, but told them, as my ammunition was not in abundance, it was neceffary to be fparing of it, that a fufficient referve might be made for the more effential fervices of war. This was acquiefced in, and in future huntings, I was to ufe the bow and
fpear

spear in their manner; after having learned the ufe of them by repeated exercife. Ulopeia and I were become intimate friends; at firft, gratitude to my benefactor, made me fhew him a greater attachment than any other warrior; but, upon knowing him better, I found him worthy of my warmeft affection; having a generofity and humanity uncommon to favages. For two days before we were to fet out on our hunting, he fnuffed up the powder of an herb, which occafioned a difcharge from his nofe, and defired me to do the fame: I complied, but not without afking him for what purpofe it was ufed. He replied, to quicken my fmelling faculty, that the fcent of the animals we were to deftroy, might be more ftrongly impreffed on our nofes. This furprifed me me greatly; what, thought I! have thefe people the faculty of hounds or pointers? If they have, it is very convenient, as I fee none of thefe animals in this country, and believe it would not be an eafy matter for them to procure a breed.

When we fet out, we kept together for fome time, and it much furprifed and diverted me, to fee them fnuffing up the fcent from the ground; but foon after, every one went off in full cry, after the track they had fixed on, like a pack of beagles; and we faw no more of them till night, when we met at the general rendezvous. Ulopeia did not hunt that day, but kept with me, to obferve the effects of my gun; and to conduct me to the rendezvous. Fortunately I was very fuccefsful,

exerting

exerting myfelf, that my new friends and countrymen might not refufe me their efteem; I did not mifs a fhot. Six deer and four foxes were killed by me alone; befides many birds which were fhot while they were flying; which Ulopeia chiefly admired, as being uncommon with their weapons. We were obliged to leave the greateft part of our dead game, at certain ftations appointed for that purpofe; and repaired to the rendezvous, where all the hunters collected themfelves. The whole converfation turned on the different fuccefs of each particular, and mine was allowed to be far fuperior to any other. A deer and fome of the birds which I had fhot, were dreffed for our fuppers, when, after eating heartily, we all went to fleep round a great fire, till day-light next morning.

ing. The ammunition which I had allotted for this experiment being all fpent, the reft of the time we were out, I attended and obferved my friend Ulopeia. It was really wonderful to fee how he purfued the fcent, with an undeviating certainty and perfevering ardour till he deftroyed the animal with his weapons. I often tried if my nofe could difcover any thing particular to me, but was always difappointed. I therefore concluded, that theirs muft either be ftrengthened by conftant ufe, or formed differently from the reft of mankind. We continued out on this hunting occupation (for it is to them of the greateft confequence) for ten days; and having got a fufficient ftock of provifions, returned home; giving ourfelves no trouble about our game; that was left to the women, who
came

came daily to the places appointed in the woods for leaving it; and with great labour carried it home to the villages. Indeed, that part of the fpecies is very hardly treated by thefe people; they are looked upon as infinitely inferior in their nature to the men; and though of a fize and ftrength lefs fit for laborious offices, all the drudgeries of life fall to their fhare; in fhort, they are ufed like perfect flaves. This may be feen in their appearance; they have a languid tamenefs in their looks, which fhows they expect no court paid to them by the other fex, but that their lot is implicitly to ferve and obey.

A life of perfect idlenefs fucceeded our hunting; lying afleep on the ground, or converfing with one another, and fometimes dancing, filled
up

up our time; but the women were never suffered to join in our recreations. One day Uncomia propofed to me that I fhould take a wife; your conftitution muft certainly require one, faid he, fo young as you are; and fhe will be of great ufe in ferving and waiting on you. My reply was, that marriage was a very ferious affair; and that an engagement for life fhould not be entered into, without a mutual affection, and a prudence of character in the female. ——Whilft I was going on, he burft out a laughing; and faid, What is all this you are talking of? you are making marriage a very ferious thing indeed; but we love freedom too well to be fo fhackled. With us it is the loofeft knot poffible; a man takes the woman who beft pleafes him, to

live

live with him while she continues so to do; and when that no longer is the case, he turns her off and takes another. They are true to one another while together; and when they part, the woman is not liked the worse for having been another's.

The children are the father's care, or rather that of the nation; for if their father should die, they are not the less taken care of. You see, continued he, there is nothing formidable in it; and as we think it every man's duty to raise children for the state, I would advise you to it. Examine the women that are not engaged, and whichever of them pleases you best, you may have; with us they have no liberty of refusing.

After weighing this affair with some attention, it appeared to me, that,

that, as I had voluntarily entered into this fociety, I ought to fulfil the duties of it; efpecially as there was nothing burthenfome in them. I then examined the women who were unengaged, with more attention than I had hitherto done, and fixed on one called Tauropa, as being the leaft difagreeable in my eyes. This being known, a hut was prepared for us; and my friends prefented me with the few neceffaries I wanted for houfe-keeping; fo that without further ceremony I took her home. My choice was fo fortunate, that I never had occafion to repent, or change; for though not handfome to my European tafte, fhe was very good tempered and obedient; two qualifications much more material in that ftate. She had alfo another excellent quality, in common with all the women

men of that country; which was cleanliness, both in her own person, and every thing about the house. In this, they certainly far excel our English women, and perhaps all Europeans (if the Dutch be not excepted, amongst whom I never was). What I conceived to be the reason of it, was the very acute sense of smelling, with which the men were endued.

Though I daily applied close to my exercises, of shooting with a bow and arrow at a mark, brandishing my spear, and handling the Patapatoo with dexterity, a great deal of spare time lay upon my hands. This was usually spent in conversation with my friends, or the other warriors; the topicks of which, generally turned on the customs and manners of my country;

or

or inquiries concerning particulars relating to theirs, of which I was not yet well informed. Sometimes religion was fpoke of, and I learned, that their adoration was paid to the fun and moon; but without any images of them in their houfes (as they had thefe luminaries themfelves fo often in view), or facrifices offered at their altars. I took fome pains to perfuade them to turn their worfhip, from the creature to the creator; and endeavoured to explain to them, the myfteries of the Chriftian Religion, but could not poffibly make them underftand me.

Their anfwers and objections were fometimes fo fhrewd, that it might be looked on, as impiety in me to relate them; and therefore I fhall only fay, that they often puzzled me

(who

(who am indeed no deep divine) to anfwer them.

I had taken notice, that the Olfactarians had fome coarfe woollen cloths for their winter drefs (though I have feen none of this fort in London amongft the curiofities brought from thence), and it came into my thoughts one day, to afk where they got the wool; as I faw no fheep in the country. The anfwer made me was, that part of the fea-coaft was in their teritories; and the inhabitants next it were fifhermen as well as huntfmen. That there were many large canoes belonging to the nation, which held between twenty and thirty men upon occafion: two or three of thefe were fent twice a year loaded with deer, foxes, and other fkins, to a country about a week's

fail

fail from thence, where they exchanged them for wool; and the skins of a large animal which these people had, of which they made soles for their shoes. I cannot help owning, that though my situation was far from disagreeable at that time, yet this account caused a longing in me, to see a people, who I thought must be more civilised than those with whom I at present lived.

While we were thus passing our time in sloth and idleness, (for a savage's life is always in extremes), a great alarm was spread over all the nation, that six large canoes full of Carnovirrians, had made a descent in the country, under the command of their famous chief Tearabolo, and were carrying destruction wherever they came. Every one now ran to arms,

arms, the war dance was seen in every village, and my benefactor Ucomia cried out, Now the time is come, when you may have your revenge of those men-eaters who devoured your countrymen. I replied, That I was now a member of another nation which was attacked, and whom it was my duty to defend, at the hazard of my life. He then said to me, What would your countrymen do in our present situation? I answered, It was impossible to say that, as different men judged differently; and one man better than another, according as he had sense and judgment. But what is your opinion said he, of the conduct we should hold in driving them out of our country? Not to drive them out at all, rejoined I. What do you mean;

let me underſtand you?— Give me leave firſt to aſk you a queſtion or two?—As many as you pleaſe. My firſt then is, ſaid I, If your nation can follow the ſcent of men, and diſtinguiſh your friends from your foes, as well as they do that of deer and other game?——His anſwer being in the affirmative:—My ſecond then is, If your enemies are endued with the ſame powers?——He replied, They were not.

As that is the caſe, ſaid I, to prevent continual attacks of a ſimilar kind, from ſo inhuman a people; thoſe now in our country ſhould be utterly deſtroyed. And the way to effect that, in my opinion, is to cut off their retreat. In the firſt place then, march a ſtrong party to the ſeaſide, where their canoes are lying, and

and burn them; and after leaving a sufficient body to prevent others from landing; hunt them down like any other game, till they are utterly deftroyed. In doing this, you will have infinite advantages, from your fuperiority of numbers, and the excellency of your nofes. He relifhed my advice, and faid, he would propofe it in the council of their chiefs. But Bowmania, faid he, do not fear that I fhould take the honour of it to myfelf; depend upon it they fhall know its author, and your zeal for the fervice of our country. My advice was taken, and gained me confiderable reputation, for I was immediately elected, by unanimous confent, a chief of the third order; and went fecond in command to put the firft part of it in execution,

the

the burning the canoes. Tlulapeia commanded this detachment, and as he was my very good friend, we had no difagreement in the execution of our orders. What made our fuccefs the more eafy and certain was, they had left them but flenderly guarded, not expecting fo bold a ftroke. We furprifed the guard,—— took them prifoners, and with all expedition fet the veffels in a blaze. What gave us great fatisfaction on the execution of this fmall exploit was, that two others full of men were within two leagues of the coaft, coming to join their friends; but feeing the canoes in a flame, firft ftopped to confult what they fhould do, and foon after changed their courfe and returned. Tlulapeia with a fufficient force remained on the

fea-sea-coast, to watch the enemy's motions by water, according to his orders; and I with the remainder marched back to the head-quarters to give an account of our success; and to receive farther commands. My account of our success gave great satisfaction to the generality of the nation; though there were not wanting some, who were of opinion, that their retreat should not in this manner have been cut off; as it would make them more desperate and furious, and consequently the war more bloody. I was now raised, by universal consent, to be a chief of the second order, and had the command of forty men.

The whole fighting men of the nation being now in arms, they were divided into large parties, under different

ferent leaders; and each had a separate diſtrict allotted him, in which he was to act offenſively againſt the enemy. But they were permitted, in caſes of neceſſity, to go into a neighbouring one, either to avoid the enemy, if too powerful for them, or to aſſiſt their friends. As I had a great ambition to be oppoſed to that formidable chief Tearabola, I requeſted that no particular diſtrict ſhould be allotted me; but that I might be at liberty to purſue him wherever I pleaſed. This was eaſily granted me, as he was become very formidable to the nation in general. We marched then into the woods in large diviſions, and were not to ſubdivide, till our noſes informed us that the enemy had firſt done ſo. To deſcribe every ſkirmiſh which happened in the

the woods, small parties against small parties, and man to man, in the course of a war of above three weeks continuance (if it were possible), would be tedious. Suffice it to say, that in them the greater part of the enemy were killed or taken prisoners; not without the loss of many brave men on our side. At last Tearabola, with only twenty-five of his men, were hemmed in on every side; when a dreadful battle began. He and his brave followers, like so many tigers surrounded by a multitude of huntsmen, turned upon their enemies with all the fierceness of these animals. To escape they saw was impossible, and to yield, unbecoming their courage; the only thing they had then left, was to sell their lives as dear as they could. Tearabola

bola did not that day bely the character he had so long acquired, of invincible courage. My dear friend Ulopeia fell by his spear; and his father, my great benefactor, was obliged to retire from the combat, by a wound in his leg. My resentment was heightened by these accidents; I presented my piece loaded with my last charge of powder and ball, and took such good aim, or was so fortunate as to pierce Tearabolo's heart; whose furious soul left his body with a convulsive spring.

His followers seeing him fall, were daunted; and being worn out with their long defence, made but feeble efforts, and were soon all cut in pieces. Thus having the honour of some share in the termination of this war, I was raised to the dignity of Chief
of

of the firſt order. But my ſatisfaction on this occaſion was greatly leſſened, by my dear friend's death, and his father's wound. The thorough revenge of my dear countrymen, however (notwithſtanding what religion might inculcate), was certainly not altogether indifferent to me on this occaſion. Though from ſome words which fell from Uncomia, I believed the Olfactarians were not cannibals; yet I never could prevail on myſelf to aſk the queſtion; thinking it better to continue in uncertainty, than learn an unpleaſing truth: but now I had many opportunities of being convinced they were not; as graves were dug, and their enemies buried in them. But though they ſpared their dead enemies, they had no mercy on thoſe who

who fell into their hands alive. To enumerate the various tortures they were put to, before they were flain; and the fortitude feemingly more than human, with which they were fupported; would only fhock the reader's humanity, and fhall therefore be paffed over.

We returned to our habitations, where there was great rejoicings for the termination of the war; but the families who had loft their warriors kept retired, brooding over their forrows, that they might not interrupt the general joy. My benefactor, who was one of thofe (and alfo confined with his wound), received me with tears in his eyes; faying, I had loft a true friend, but as he died in his country's fervice, was more to be envied than lamented. I learned
from

from him that his wound was very painful, the whole member being greatly fwelled, and that he had very little hopes of recovery. I examined the part, and though unfkilled in furgery, more than I had accidentally feen practifed by our own furgeons on board, I was refolved to attempt his relief. I gathered fome herbs, and made a fomentation and poultice, which foon eafed his pain; the fwelling alfo decreafed by degrees, and the wound advanced daily towards a cure. My fatisfaction on this account was more real than that for the dignities which fortune had heaped on me; for I eafily perceived they were not unattended with envy. We had not been long at home, before it became neceffary to go on a hunting-party, as our

our old men, women and children, had been on very short allowance in our absence. It was mentioned before, that my last charge of ammunition was expended; I must now therefore betake myself to their weapons; at which (though I had not neglected exercising with them constantly before the war) I certainly was very inferior to the natives. Add to that, my want of a nose; and it may easily be imagined, I should make a very bad figure. But I flattered myself, that the great services I had so lately done my country, and the being unpractised in their arms, would sufficienly apologize for me. How little did I know mankind? A few brilliant actions are soon forgot, if people's memories are not frequently refreshed with
some

some of the same kind, or even of greater lustre: but a reverse, however little merited, is with great difficulty got over, and generally damns our fame irrecoverably.

The war had so destroyed and disturbed the game, that it was extremely scarce; and consequently our hunting very unsuccessful; mine was remarkably so: famine appeared unavoidable; which so chagrined mens minds, that my laurels (for want of some fresh exploit), withered daily. They even openly blamed my bold advice in the beginning of the war, as the chief cause of the misfortunes which threatened them, and I saw myself in the utmost danger of being degraded.

This country, and way of life, which hitherto had been agreeable
enough

enough to me, changed at once its appearance: I became thoughtful and melancholy; wishing for a good opportunity of quitting it for ever. The country from which they brought the wool, then recurred to my memory: I began seriously to think of the means of putting in execution a scheme I formed of visiting it by the first ships, which would not be long before they sailed. Uncomia seeing me so much changed since our return home, kindly enquired the reason of it; when I frankly told him, that I had reason to complain of the warriors, for blaming me for an event that could not possibly have been foreseen. They also slight me, continued I, because I have not been able to acquire in a few days, the use of their arms to as

great

IN OLFACTARIA. 113

great perfection as they have, by the practice of their whole lives. Besides, (I still continued) nature has given them such an advantage over me in their scenting faculty, that there is no possibility of my ever equalling them as a hunter; and I should therefore be glad to serve the nation in any other capacity. That I understood some great canoes would soon sail for Auditante, to exchange their skins for wool and other commodities of that country. And I believed, as my education had been for a sea-life (which indeed had brought me into that part of the world), that I was better qualified than most others, for carrying on that traffic with the Auditantines; and should offer my services to the nation, if he approved of it. He replied, that he had no

I objection

objection to it, but the lofing my company for fo long a time; and if I was refolved on the voyage, he would ufe all his influence with the National Council in my favour, when it was laid before them. Accordingly very little oppofition was made, and I was appointed to the command of one of the canoes. Two other chiefs of the fame rank (who fortunately were my friends), were alfo fixed on for the other two; and in a fhort time we fet out for our ftation, to fuperintend the loading of the fkins, which were carried by the women from all the villages to Tahuta where the canoes lay. The veffels were obliged to be victualled principally with fifh, on account of the fcarcity of land animals; and we ftowed our water in

jars,

jars, which the women had ingenuity enough to make. Each canoe had twelve men on board, befides three officers; which confifted of a chief of the firft, fecond, and third orders.

Before I left our village Manuhu, I fent my wife Tewropa home to her friends till my return (which however I did not intend), and left with her a prefent to the nation, to keep me in their remembrance. I hope if it proves a boy, that he will make a good warrior; but am very much afraid he will have no nofe, which may be a great lofs to him. With my friend Uncomia, whom I principally regretted to leave; my fufee was intrufted by way of a relic, as it could be of no father ufe to me, for want of ammunition. And a few nails, and other European baubles,

bles, which still remained in my possession, were distributed amongst my other friends.

On July 26th, 1774, we set sail with a fair wind; and I found these people very expert at working their canoes. The weather kept moderate, so that we had little difficulty of keeping company; and we seldom lost sight of land for any length of time. At last, on the tenth day from the time we sailed, the coast of Auditante appeared to our view; and on the eleventh we came to an anchor in the river of Seripante.

CHAP.

CHAP. IV.

Seripante, a Factory of Bonhommican Merchants. The Author and his Colleagues live at their houses. Very fair traders. Visit the tents of the natives. He learns in a short time, the Bonhommican and Auditante languages. Makes a speech to the Olfactarian Chiefs at taking leave of them. By invitation, lives sometime at a Horde of the Auditantines. Falls in love. Lucky discovery which cures him of it. The fleet from Ludorow arrives. The fair held in consequence of it. The Author embarks in it, on its return. Arrives at Ludorow.

AS soon as the canoes were moored, Teutopeia, Nicophera, and myself (the three chiefs of the first order), went up to the town in our small canoes. It lay about a league higher up the river, and the country on each side exhibited a very agreeable prospect, of green hills covered with flocks of sheep, and herds of black cattle: I even thought there appeared horses, and animals like camels or dromaderys. When we approached the town, I was delighted to see that the houses were built of stone, and were several stories high, and began to think myself again in Europe. We were met at our landing by the merchants, with whom the nation had been accustomed to deal; who received us with great civility and respect, entertaining us by turns at their houses, and gave us also invitations to lye at them, as we could not otherwise be so well accommodated.

The

The merchant with whom I lived was called Ouragow; he seemed about forty, and a man of a grave, though sweet and affable deportment. He understood the Olfactarian language well enough to do business in it, and carry on a conversation. Curiosity soon drew me to view the town; it was but of a small size, consisting only of about two hundred houses; fifty of which were large, and had still larger warehouses adjoining to them. But what most surprised me, was, to find the houses of these merchants, furnished with every thing necessary for the conveniency, and even the elegancy of life; it was, it is true, in a simple plain taste, and very different from what I had ever seen before; but answered the end as well

well when one became accustomed to them. They had also woollen, linen, and other cloths; and even silk stuffs: very good wines were produced at table, as well as excellent bread; and their windows were glazed. These discoveries gave me infinite pleasure; I flattered myself that my troubles were at an end; and if I should never have the happiness of visiting Old England, my life would at least be passed in a more agreeable manner, than my most sanguine hopes had ever conceived.

Having rested and amused ourselves for a day or two, we thought of business; and that which first offered, was, to get our goods lodged in a warehouse, to be ready for bartering. This was immediately set about, and
the

the small canoes were kept constantly employed in it till all was landed. After that, the chiefs of the second order came up to town also, with some of the men, leaving only the chief of the third order, with three men, on board of each canoe; and these were relieved every six or seven days, that all might have a little pleasure; the second chief's relieving the third.

When we had been there five or six days, Ouragow and I happening to be alone together, he bethought himself of asking me (what he said he had intended ever since we came); from what country I claimed my birth; for he could plainly see from my complexion, my features, and manners, that I was not an Olfactarian; besides, said he, you have been too

too wife to disfigure your face with horrid tattooings, and to load your nofe and ears with fuch frightful ornaments. Having no reafon to conceal any thing, I gave him a faithful account of all my adventures, and even of my defign of never returning to Olfactaria ; faying, Now I had got into a civilifed country, things might take a turn in my favour; and I hoped to find fome means of earning an honeft living. When I had finifhed my narration, he fat fometime filent; and then cried out, What wonders have you told me! How furprifing is it to me, who am of a trading nation, to learn, that there are people on the other fide the globe, who have carried navigation to fuch a height, as to fend fhips all over the face of the

earth,

earth, where seas will bear them, and ice not obstruct their passage; to discover new countries and new people! But, said he, is it meerly curiosity that prompts your king to these expensive researches? or has he trade or conquest in view? I replied, That trade or conquest at such an immense distance from his own dominions could never answer the expence of either; and did he reckon it for nothing to a great, opulent, and philosophic nation, to have the honour of ascertaining to the rest of the northern world, whether the southern hemisphere was equally balanced by a large continent, as the learnedest Geographers had conjectured. That near three hundred years ago, a great geographer and navigator, meerly from

con-

conjectures, had discovered a continent almost as large as the rest of the known world, lying only at a thousand leagues distance from the rest of Europe. Upon a second consideration, rejoined he, it appears praise-worthy, though at first view it had, I own, a romantic air: But what success had you met with before you was separated from the ship? We had sailed (returned I) half round the southern hemisphere in very high latitudes, without meeting with any land, but had been obstructed by numerous and large islands of ice; which made us conclude, that if there was a continent, it must be so near the pole, as to be uninhabitable. I am surprised, said he, that you missed it; but if your ships, after a farther search, are not so fortunate to succeed, it may be reserved for you to make that discovery, if ever you have the happiness to get home to your own country; for you are now in a fair way of getting intelligence of, and in all probability of seeing it. You both surprise and rejoice me, said I, to hear there is a southern continent which there is a possibility of my seeing; and likewise that I am got into a country which has an extensive trade, as it is in that way my talents can best distinguish themselves. But what is the reason, continued I, that I saw no ships in the river? You have misunderstood me, answered he; I am of a trading nation, 'tis true, but not of this where I now live. The inhabitants of Serepante are all natives of the island of Bonhommica, settled

on

on this coaft as a factory, for the conveniency of commerce with the natives. And who are the natives, rejoined I? This large country, faid he, being peculiarly fuited for pafture only, is occupied by wandering tribes, who live in tents, and change from one place to another, as it beft fuits their flocks and herds; no one having the property of the foil, but the firft comer enjoys it during his abode. And the country being very extenfive in proportion to the number of its inhabitants, there feldom arifes any caufe of difpute on that head. They are a handfome, robuft people, continued he; and fome of them have immenfe flocks and herds, with children and fervants fo numerous, that their encampments look like fmall towns. But they are fo idle,

that,

that, though they have time enough on their hands, they will not be at the trouble of manufacturing their own wool for their clothing, or doing any earthly thing but what neceffity obliges them to. So that, all their wool, and other produce of their cattle, is exchanged with us, for our manufactures; which are brought annually in a fmall fleet to this port; where a fair is kept for a month, and reforted to from all parts of the country. Thofe who have not fupplied themfelves fufficiently at the fair, have recourfe to us from time to time; there being always great quantities of goods in our warehoufes. Our converfation now turning on the caufes of induftry and idlenefs in nations, he obferved, that the gift with which

bounteous

bounteous Nature had favoured the Olfactarians, in the improved faculty of smelling (which he had learned only from my narrative), seemed to be of great use to them in providing for their subsistence. But, on the contrary, continued he, a gift of a similar kind which the Auditantines enjoy in their sense of hearing, had a very different effect. For they had such exquisite enjoyment in Musical performances, and the hearing of love elegies, and other pieces of well wrote poetry read, that their whole time was spent in such fooleries. These improved faculties have however their alloy; for as the Olfactarians are easily offended with the least unpleasing smell, so the Auditantines suffer excruciating anguish from any very loud or harsh sound:

It

It is happy for them (continued he) that it never thunders in this country; and the moſt diſagreeable thing their way of life ſubjects them to, is the bray of an aſs; but they take care to keep them always at a ſufficient diſtance from their tents. The ſmalleſt matter however hurts their nice ears, ſuch as an inſtrument not thoroughly in tune, or playing out of time; and the ſame of a voice with reſpect to the latter. This long converſation was concluded, by an offer from him of getting me a paſſage to Bonhommica if I choſe it, when the fleet returned from this country after the Fair; and likewiſe to recommend me warmly to all his friends in that country. This kind offer I gratefully accepted, and begged he would put me in a way of learning the language in the mean time, that I might not be wholly at a lofs in that refpect. This he immediately complied with, and put me under the tuition of one of the book-keepers in his compting-houfe; faying at the fame time, that he could alfo inftruct me in the Auditantine, which would qualify me to vifit that people, who were very hofpitable, if my curiofity led me to it, and for which I fhould have fufficient time. This propofal was much to my mind, and I immediately applied myfelf with great induftry to acquire thofe languages.

In the mean time, nothing was neglected on my part to affift my colleagues in tranfacting the bufinefs of the Olfactarians; and in every particular I had the fatisfaction to find our merchants acted like honeft men and

and fair traders. Far were they from defigning to take any advantage of my ignorance, or that of the favages, in the value of the goods to be exchanged. This was what at leaft then appeared to me, and I had reafon afterwards to be convinced of the truth of it. As our goods were neither bulky, nor confifted of many articles, which were to be exchanged betwixt the merchants and us, matters were not long in adjufting; and our wool, leather, &c. were begun to be put on board the canoes.

In all thefe tranfactions, I took particular care that Seropa, the fecond in command on board mine, fhould be prefent, and thoroughly inftructed in them; as he was probably to have the command of her home, it was his proper bufinefs to fuperintend the relading.

The reader will naturally imagine, that I did not long neglect viewing a country, which gave me so much pleasure in the approaching. In company with some of the merchants or brother savages, I frequently walked, or rode out, many miles into different parts of it. Every thing appeared gay and smiling to me, who had been so long unaccustomed to such prospects. The height of the hills varied in different parts; in some they rose nearly to mountains, and in others descended almost to a flat country: but all were covered with a pleasing verdure. I saw no woods, but there were every where many clumps of trees, scattered about in an irregular manner; and abundance of small rivulets of the purest water, which was not only an ornament to

to the country, but of the greateſt ufe to man and beaſt. The ſheep which fed on thoſe delighful hills, were of the fame ſpecies with theſe I had feen at the Cape of Good Hope, with large heavy tails, and were innumerable. The horſes were beautiful, and reſembled in their ſhape, the Arabians and Barbs which I had often feen in Yorkſhire. Black cattle were of two kinds, fome reſembling ours in Europe, and others of the buffalo ſpecies. I had never feen camels or dromedaries before, except in painting. Their aſſes were large, and the Mules ſtill more fo. We often went to their encampments, and when the merchants were with us, viſited the natives. Every place reſounded with the pleaſing melody of muſical inſtruments and harmo-
nious

nious voices*. Some of these encampments, as was said before, covered a great deal of ground; and contained some hundreds of people, besides horses, camels, &c. which were fed with cut grass. Behind the tents stood covered waggons, in which they transported their women, and the furniture of their tents, when they changed their stations. A peaceful camp, breathing nothing but harmony, was to me a sight perfectly new and engaging.

The Auditantines are generally tall, not very fair, but of a graceful appearance and very polite: Their dress is something betwixt the Asiatic and

---

* He look'd, and saw a spacious plain, whereon
Were tents of various hue; by some were herds
Of cattle grazing; others whence the sound
Of instruments, that made melodious chime,
Was heard, of harp——
   Milton's Paradise Lost, Book xi. line 556.

European; very easy and becoming; made of woollen, cotton, or silk stuffs; according to the age, sex and rank of the wearers. On the whole, I did not seem to be amongst wandering shepherds, but in the court of one of the Patriarchs we read of in Scripture, where they were king, priest, and prophet. I conceived so great a desire to be better acquainted with these people, that I was unhappy till I had learned their language. This I had often declared to Ouragow and the other merchants, at the same time acquainting them of my passion for music, and being an indifferent performer on the German Flute. One day when we were at Venerantes Horde (as I may call it), Our gow presented me to him in a particular manner; letting him know my great admiration of their way of life, as

well

well as being a paffionate lover of mufic, and a tolerable performer on the German Flute; not forgetting to acquaint him of my coming from a far country on the other fide of the world. The venerable old man received me with great affability and politenefs; and gave me an invitation to come and ftay fome time with him. This I firmly refolved to accept of, as foon as the canoes were gone, and I had made myfelf proficient enough in their language to be underftood.

When we had been above eight weeks at Seripante, and the canoes ready to fail, I fpoke to my colleagues Teutopeia and Nicophora in this manner;

"My friends, I do not intend returning with you to Olfactaria; and honeftly honestly own, that I solicited this voyage with that design. When your nation did me the honour of adopting me, I never meant to abridge myself of the liberty which nature gave me, of changing my situation, whenever it was agreeable or convenient for me. While I have been in your society, my utmost endeavours have been used to serve it; and sometimes with such success, that the nation raised me, step by step, to its chief honours and distinctions. This I own was more than I deserved, a stranger as I was; but these honours with which they were pleased unanimously to dignify me in so rapid a manner, created much envy, and laid the foundation for the rancorous hatred which many bear me; without having cause that

I know

I know for it, but their own bad hearts. Thofe enemies of mine, it is plain, will never reft, till they have got me degraded from my prefent high ftation in the ftate, and which they may eafily effect; fince I can no longer ferve them with fuch eclat as formerly, from having expended all my ammunition in their fervice. I therefore propofe to free myfelf from their machinations, by refigning into your hands thefe fo much envied honours, which I defire you will faithfully deliver (as near as you can in my own words), to the national council; returning them my moft unfeigned thanks for all their favours." When I had finifhed, my colleagues expreffed great concern for my intention of leaving them; but owned, that every thing I had

I had said was true; and wished me happy wherever fortune should carry me. I then asked them, If they thought any other of the chiefs of the second order, fitter to succeed me in the command of the canoe than Seropa, whose right it seemed to be; and they answering in the negative, Seropa was sent for, and acquainted with it. After this, I demanded of them, in presence of some of the merchants and all of the chiefs, If they had any fault to find with my transactions or behaviour, since we left Olfactaria; which they declaring they had not: I embraced them, and took a last farewel; desiring their kind remembrance, and that of all my friends, but particularly that they would make my grateful respects and good wishes known to my benefactor Uncomia.

When

When the canoes were gone, my friend Ouragow made me a prefent of a compleat drefs in the Bonhommican mode; faying, as I was no longer a favage, it was proper to leave off the appearance of one. The goodnefs of this worthy man truly charmed me, and I felt all the gratitude fuch benefits demanded. It is not to be imagined, but that two people living in the fame houfe together for fome months (as Ouragow and I did), muft have had many converfations, which for brevity's fake fhall be omitted; and I fhall only mention in general, fome informations I got from him, and opinions of his upon fubjects relating to my own country.

With refpect to the great fouthern continent, he affured me there certainly

tainly was one; and that the Bonhommicans carried on a confiderable trade to one of its kingdoms; but that he never had been there, nor could he tell me in what longitude and latitude it lay.

He alfo informed me, that the Auditantines were idolaters, and facrificed to idols.

He did not explain himfelf fufficiently on the Bonhommican religion, as he faid I would learn it better from the priefts when I went to that Ifland; but only affured me, that the principal tenet of it was the unity of the deity.

His opinion of the chriftian religion was a very favourable one, though I could not make him comprehend many parts of it; he wifhed to fee our facred books, that he might examine

examine it; for, he said, a religion which recommended so pure a morality, must have a divine origin.

Two things (with respect to our naval discoveries) seemed to give him the greatest satisfaction to be informed of, as they might be immediately useful to his own countrymen; these were, the method of preventing the scurvy in long voyages, and the art of distilling seawater to make it fresh. These, he said, were discoveries that did honour to human nature; the truth of which he could not doubt, from the length of the voyages performed by the discoverers.

I had now made a considerable progress in the two languages, which for some time had taken up my attention, particularly in the Auditantine, as

I had moſt immediate occaſion for it; but as the natives had ſuch nice ears, I was very diffident in ſpeaking it before them. That I might improve myſelf, and at the ſame time obſerve what effect my pronunciation had upon their nice organs, I uſed to walk in the fields, and ſpeak to all the menial ſhepherds, and others of low rank. At firſt they were very ſenſibly hurt; but being extremely good-natured people, they endeavoured to conceal it: by degrees, as I improved, they ſeemed leſs ſo; and, in a ſhort time, little, if any thing at all.

Before I ſet out on my viſit, Ouragow cautioned me againſt falling in love; Take care of your heart, ſaid he, in the company of ſo many charmers; and conſtantly recollect, when you find yourſelf in danger, that

that thefe women are idolaters; not forgetting the great fouthern continent.

My new drefs had altered me fo much, that Venerante did not at firft know me; but, as foon as he learned who I was, received me with great kindnefs and hofpitality. The whole horde indeed did the fame; which then confifted of above one hundred perfons, of both fexes and of all ages (exclufive of fervants and flaves). Befides, there were near as many in fmall camps on the fkirts of the ground, which their flocks and herds at prefent occupied. Thefe were moftly defcended from his own perfon; for polygamy is allowed of by them, and they marry in degrees of kindred, which are forbidden amongft chriftians. I was told by
one

one of his fons, that he had fixty thoufand fheep, five thoufand black cattle, three thoufand horfes, two thoufand camels, one thoufand fhe affes, and fifty he ones, and one thoufand mules; fo that he was by far richer than Job, who was the richeft man in all the eaft in thofe days.

We paffed our time in a continual round of what is called pleafures; fo that if idlenefs and conftant dif- fipation conftitute happinefs, thefe are the happieft of any people in the world. The large encampment which I only faw, was of an oval form; in the center of which, was a fuite of very large tents at fome diftance from one another, lined with cotton cloth; and around them were fmall ones for fleeping in, dreffing, and other offices.

offices. When we were not at meals; parties were formed in thefe large tents according to people's fancies. Some read love elegies to an audience round them, or fung tender fongs; others had concerts of mufic which were truly ravifhing. Tender and amorous converfation fuited the lovers beft. And dancing to the lively airs of the pipe and tabor, was moft agreeable to the gay and lively.

Their language is the fofteft that can be imagined, and in the women's mouths, truly enchanting; efpecially when fet to mufic, which it is peculiarly calculated for. That mufic is fimple and pathetic; they like better what affects the heart, than pleafes the fancy. The inftruments which they have, are of the fimpleft kind; befides the pipe and tabor already

already mentioned, harps, lutes, and flutes, compofe the whole of their ſtock. Though the whole people have the moſt critical ears, every one has not a voice; that gift however is much more common here, than elſewhere: for there is ſcarcely a young woman or boy but has, and many of them are ſuperlatively fine.

Their tables are plentifully ſupplied with the produce of their flocks and herds, in all the ſimplicity of cookery. Milk furniſhes them with feveral agreeable diſhes, befides butter and cheeſe; and I muſt obſerve, that, like the Tartars, they prefer horfe fleſh to beef: I taſted it, and fairly own, could ſcarcely diſtinguiſh the difference. The only things for ſubſiſtance which they are obliged to get from the Bonhommicans, are corn

corn and wine; the firſt they grind in quearns (as they do ſtill in many parts of Ireland), and then make it into bread; the laſt is only uſed on extraordinary occaſions, as a fermented liquor made of mare's milk, and a kind of mead, are their ordinary drinks.

They have images of two different gods of very rude ſculpture, to which they offer ſacrifices. Theſe idols have ſome reſemblance to the Apollo and Pan of the antients, at leaſt the one had a lyre and the other a pipe, on which they were in the attitude of playing. The government is intirely parental or patriarchal within each particular Horde, without having the leaſt connection with any other.

They

They have had writing long amongſt them, and their characters ſeemed to me ſomewhat to reſemble the Hebrew or Arabic. If the learned ſhould fancy from thence, that this people are a colony from that part of the world, I ſhall leave it to them to form conjectures, how they could poſſibly be tranſported to ſuch a diſtance.

I was for ſome days a hearer, and great admirer at all muſical entertainments; but when we became a little better acquainted, I found they had not forgot what Ouragow had ſaid of me, and had conceived great expectations of entertainment, from muſic of ſo diſtant a country. At firſt I defended myſelf from their requeſts, by the want of an inſtrument; but that would not ſerve, I muſt

I muſt make ſhift with theirs in ſome ſhape or another. Finding there was no avoiding it; I got one of their flutes of a conſtruction neareſt to a german one of any they had; and botched it up, by opening ſome holes and ſtopping up others, till at laſt I made a tolerable inſtrument of it.

As the Italian muſic is moſt admired in Europe, I began with ſome favourite airs, which were in great vogue when I left England.

The whole company were much ſurpriſed at hearing them; and owned they did not expect any thing comparable to what I had played; but, ſaid they, though theſe ſeem the ſtyle of great maſters, the ſimple and pathetic is more to our taſtes; perhaps from not knowing better. It fortunately happened that I had it in my power, besides Italian, to give them some specimens of the music of other nations in our northern world. The French was too gay; the English (except when grafted on the Italian) wanted melody; but most of the plaintive Scotch songs, and some of the Irish, were much to their tastes, and affected them wonderfully.

As I was no great proficient on my instrument, it was sometimes visible enough, that their chromatic ears were much offended by my discords, and playing out of tune; but their politeness, joined to their curiosity, made them hide it as much as possible. This talent of mine, contemptible as it was, made me a kind of favourite amongst them; they esteemed many of my songs so much, as to write them out in their manner; which, though very different from ours, was very ingenious.

I had now spent ten days with these people, and their way of life was such a contrast to what it had lately been my fortune to lead, that it could not but be agreeable to a man of my age, who was a lover of music. However my friend Ouragow's antidotes had not yet been necessary; my heart remained untouched. The time now approached when I was to give up my liberty, and burn with the most ardent passion.

A grand-daughter of Venerante returned with her parents from an out camp, and at first sight shot me through and through. She appeared to be about fifteen, and (at least in my my eyes) the moſt perfect woman heaven ever made. Her form riſing a little above the middle ſize, was made in perfect proportion; and a grace and dignity attended every motion of her moſt elegant limbs. But her face; how ſhall I deſcribe her face? to the moſt regular and beautiful features, were joined ſuch modeſty and ſweetneſs, that it was irreſiſtible. Add to all theſe, the moſt enchanting voice, far ſurpaſſing any thing I had ever heard; and judge of my condition. For ſome days I admired at a diſtance, without preſuming to have the leaſt hope of pleaſing ſuch an angelic creature. But Venerante having been pleaſed with my European ſongs, deſired one day to hear my adventures; and as he doated on Imoina (ſo the

charming

charming maid was called), could not bear fhe fhould be long from him; fhe was therefore obliged to become one of my conftant hearers. The fatisfaction of having her near me, and to hear my difafters, was great; and fometimes I thought fhe pitied them like Defdemona in the play. I fpun out my narrative to continue that fatisfaction, and by degrees fhe became lefs referved; but though I was never happy when from her, a certain awe feized me whenever I attempted to difclofe my paffion.

My antidotes, befides, were not forgot; and I thus argued with myfelf. Would you then to fatisfy a prefent paffion, however violent, give up all thoughts of feeing your native country? and the great honour of dif-
covering

covering to all Europe a southern continent, which would make your name immortal? To live with idolaters a life of idleness and dissipation, having no care but for the present moment: Where polygamy is allowed, and the women (at their full liberty), indulging themselves freely in amorous conversation, probably are not very scrupulous in violating their marriage vows. On the other hand, to give up all thoughts of Imoina, and let her be possessed by another, was what I could not think of. This struggle continued for some time; I grew thoughtful, and absent, to such a degree that every one took notice of it. Some said, I was in love; others, that their company was grown tiresome to me; but Imoina was very reserved on that head. At other times I confidered, that if my fcruples fhould give way to love, and Imoina was favourable to my wifhes; what probability was there, that Trapante her father, or Venerante her grandfather, would ever confent to my having her; a ftranger, of a different religion, and poor. Thus did love and reafon combat in my breaft; and to my fhame I fay it, reafon made but a bad defence. The firft fign of victory which appeared on the fide of love, was a copy of verfes of my compofing; I got a friend to fet them to mufic; and though they were probably very indifferent, every body applauded them; being willing I fuppofe to encourage a beginner. And though it was now plain where my attachment was, no one feemed difpleafed

pleafed with it, even Imoina was not more fhy than ufual. This encouraged me to fpeak: I foon met with a favourable opportunity, and my addreffes were well received, confidering the modefty of the fex. The ice being now broke, I had as many opportunities of pleading my paffion as could be defired; and foon had the pleafure of being told, that I was not difagreeable to her. She now indulged me in all the innocent liberties I prefumed to take; which made the time pafs away in a kind of intoxication, which nothing but enjoyment, or the difcovery I afterwards made, could have put an end to.

While my thoughts were employed on completing my happinefs, by endeavouring to obtain the confent of
thofe

those on whom she depended, but delayed from day to day, from a consciousness that I was acting wrong, and the fear of a refusal; something appeared to me to be going on betwixt her, and her brother-in-law Amarante, which seemed very suspicious. My jealousy was roused, and I watched all their motions narrowly; several days passed on, before my doubts were cleared up: at last, one evening they slipped out, one after another, from one of the great tents, in the midst of a very interesting piece of music: I immediately followed, and traced them into a bed-tent. This was sufficient for me, Cupid immediately took his flight from my bosom; and when I saw her return to the tent, she seemed despoiled of more than half her

her charms, and not more beautiful than any other woman. I paſſed, however, a very diſagreeable night, and reſolved to quit her ſight for ever. Next morning I took leave of Venerante and his Horde, who all preſſed me to ſtay ſometime longer; but I excuſed myſelf on account of buſineſs at Seripante, and immediately ſet out for that place.

When I had given my friend Ouragow a candid relation of my amour, he congratulated me very affectionately on my eſcape; and ſaid, Young man, let this piece of experience, which was ſo near being fatal, teach you for the future, that the beſt way to avert the dangers of that powerful paſſion, is to keep out of temptation; or if unexpectedly ſurpriſed into it, to fly immediately.

The

The fleet from Bonhommica being now foon expected, I applied very clofe to perfecting myfelf in that language; fpeaking in no other, and reading feveral books concerning their hiftory, government, manners, &c. &c. which was of great advantage to me when I arrived in that country. But notwithftanding my time was pretty well filled up, the image of the beautiful Imoina would often intrude into my fancy; then would I regret that fuch external perfection was not accompanied with as beautiful a mind. My thoughts would then be led to confider, the influence of education and example upon the female manners; and my partiality for her induced me to think, that if fhe had been born an Englifh woman, and of courfe bred up up a christian, that she would have acted in a very different manner. But again reflecting on some bad characters I had known, and many that common report had held up to infamy amongst my fair countrywomen; I knew not what to think; but resolved to banish her if possible from my thoughts.

This was much assisted in a little time by the arrival of the fleet, and the Fair held in consequence of it. My curiosity first led me to examine the construction of their ships; which though far inferior to ours both in beauty of form, and neatness of workmanship, yet very much surprised me; as they promised to answer the purposes of navigation very well; and I conceived that the art of ship-building might be now in that state at Bonhommica, which it was in, in England, two centuries ago. The burthens of those now in Scripante river, seemed to be from three hundred to one hundred and fifty tons.

They had no ships of war with them as a convoy, the nation being at peace with all the world. The number of them were twenty, and their loading may easily be judged of, from what has already been said.

Nothing worth relating happened at the fair; it was held near the town, and the Auditantines came to it on horse-back, attended by covered waggons, in which was conveyed their cheese, salt butter and hides, &c. The wool was brought on camels. Some horses and mules were

were also sold by them at the Fair. No women attended them, so that there were no amusements going on, as is customary in England on these occasions; which I was very glad of.

When the Fair was over, preparations were made by the fleet for their return; and my good friend procured me a passage in the ship commanded by Tourabow, an honest plain sailor, with whom I was very well acquainted. He also gave me very warm recommendatory letters to several of his friends. When every thing was ready for sailing, he took leave of me, as if I had been his only son, expressing his ardent wishes for my welfare; and desiring I would favour him from time to time with accounts of what happened to me. I parted with that worthy man, with tears in my eyes, being much moved with the many teftimonies he had given me of his affection.

We failed from Seripante with a fair wind, and during the voyage, I was very well amufed with obferving their different manœuvres. They had difcovered the ufe of the magnet in navigation, and had clumfy mariners compaffes; but were abfolute ftrangers to the variation of the needle. Their Quadrant was alfo very defective, as was their log-line, for keeping an account of the fhip's way; and they had no other means of gueffing at the longitude. However, on the whole, they were careful, robuft, and active feamen.

Our voyage was agreeable, having fine weather, but rather too little wind. The eighteenth day, we made
the

the land of Bonhommica; the 19th, entered the river Tourorow; and the 21ſt, came to an anchor at Ludorow, the capital of the kingdom, being the 15th of January 1775.

CHAP. V.

The Author invited to reſide with a near relation of his friend at Seripante. By the means of him, and others to whom he had letters, he is preſented to the Lord Admiral, to the Lord Treaſurer, and at laſt to the Queen. She ſettles a penſion on him. He confers with Officers, Aſtronomers, Surveyors, Phyſicians, and Mechanicks, on the means of introducing the Engliſh improvements into the Bonhommican Navy. He is appointed a Poſt Captain, and is to command a ſhip of forty guns (going to the ſouthern continent), under a Commodore. Has the fitting her out in the Engliſh manner. She is much admired. The Queen dines on board of her. They ſail for Luxo-volupto. Arrive ſafely at Miro-volante.

ON our arrival in this kingdom, my eyes were delighted with the ſight of corn-fields, (as well as

paſture

pasture grounds) hedge-row inclosures, farm houses, and country seats; with the prospect of a large and populous city at a distance: In short, every thing demonstrated that I was again got into a civilised country. When we landed, Tourabow conducted me to the house of Lurgofage, a near relation of my friend; who after he had read the letter I had presented to him, clasped me in his arms, and received me in so affectionate a manner, that it plainly appeared to be no common letter of recommendation which I had delivered. He insisted on my taking up my abode with him, and always behaved to me with the warmest friendship. When I had got a little settled with him, my other letters were delivered; and every one received

received me equally well; they were all confiderable merchants, and they feemed fuch worthy and friendly people, that I thought myfelf got among a fuperior rank of beings. My time was fpent among them in the moft agreeable manner, walking over the different parts of the town, always in the company of fome one or more of their families; in dining and fupping alternately with them, and in agreeable and improving converfation. In the laft, while I informed them of particulars concerning my country, and travels; I was myfelf made acquainted with many things about theirs, which I was yet ignorant of. They were at this time governed by a Queen, named Tudorina, who was poffeffed of abilities, fteadinefs, and magnanimity, that far

furpaffed

surpassed most of the Kings her predecessors. By her prudent choice of Ministers, and the wise tenor of her administration, she had extricated herself out of many difficulties, kept her kingdom in peace, encouraged trade and manufactures, and was laying the foundation of a maritime power. All these things had their due merit, with a virtuous and sensible people; she was not only respected and obeyed, but in a manner adored by them. This was a happy conjuncture for a stranger, who wanted to be employed in the naval service. My excellent friend at Scripante, had recommended in all his letters, that they would think of the properest method of turning to my advantage, the discovery of many improvements in Navigation, and

preserving

preserving the health of sea-men, made by my countrymen, which I had it in my power to disclose; and this had very much occupied their thoughts ever since my arrival. One day when they were met at dinner at Lurgofage's upon this subject; when the affair was brought on the carpet, and different means were proposed; Minofrage said he was very well acquainted with the secretary to Howarow the Lurgow Amorow, (Lord Admiral) and if they approved, he would mention it to him; who probably would either introduce me to the Lurgow Amorow himself, or advise what should be done. This was agreed to, and two days after I had an invitation to dine at Minofrage's to meet the secretary. It may naturally be supposed he wanted

wanted to judge himself whether I merited the character had been given of me. He seemed a sensible man, and was very minute in his inquiries, especially of things in the naval department. I was very open, and explicit, and suppose his report of me was favourable; as in a day or two after, he came to Lurgofage's, and offered to introduce me to the Lurgow Amorow the next morning. That great officer was attended by some of the principal commanders, who all received me with great goodness. The conference was long, as the subject was very extensive; every particular respecting ship-building, victualing, sailing, fighting, arms, anchorage, &c. &c. was inquired into; and I gave them as satisfactory answers as my memory served me with;

telling

telling them also, what defects I had observed in the ship which brought me from Seripante, and in the manner of navigating her. Some days passed, without our hearing any thing of the result of this conference; but at last a message came from the great Burlohow, the Treasurer and first Minister, desiring to see me two days after. This we thought looked well, and I made my appearance at the time appointed. He had a winning affable address, that made you soon forget you was in the presence of the great man; but so penetrating an eye, that he looked into your very soul. He began with naval affairs, but did not confine himself to that subject; drawing me in to give an account of our wars for a century past; the expence

expence of them, how the money was raised, our public funds, national debt, &c. When I had given the best account that one so little versed in these matters was capable of; he said, that the trade of my country must be very extensive, and its opulence very great, to bear such an immense load of debt; but it was a dangerous practice, and he hoped the Bonhommicans would never be led, from any necessity of state, to begin any thing similar to it; as from the experience of my country, it appeared very difficult for a nation to extricate itself out of such a situation. He then in a very gracious manner dismissed me, promising to mention me favourably to her Majesty. I now thought there was an end to my catechisings, but was mistaken; for some time

time after, a meffage came to me from the Treafurer, defiring me to be at court on an appointed day, as the Queen wanted to fee me. I got a proper drefs made in all hafte, and attended by fome of my friends prefented myfelf. A Lurgow in waiting introduced me into her Majefty's clofet, where fhe appeared with fuch a dignity of afpect and deportment, that I was ftruck with an awe which I found it difficult to recover from. She obferved it, and putting on a milder look, faid, Stranger, I have been informed, you come from a highly civilifed country, on the other fide of the world, and that you have met with extraordinary adventures. I was curious to fee you, and hear them, therefore ordered you to appear before me; but fear nothing,
I am

I am prepoffeffed in your favour, from what my minifters have already told me, and believe you will be of ufe to me in my navy; therefore relate to me your adventures, as if you was only in company with your equals. This condefcenfion in her Majefty removed the awe that had feifed me, and I obeyed her with more refolution than I thought myfelf capable of. When I had finifhed, fhe afked me a great many queftions about Great Britain, and particularly about their Majefties, commanding me to give my real opinion of them without referve, faying, there was no danger of its ever coming to their ears. When I had complied, and given the character of them, which in my opinion, and that of all candid men, was really their due, recounting also their numerous progeny, she held up her hands in great raptures; crying out, O happy people! blessed with such a King and such a succession! but all at once she turned to me and said, are they happy? I answered, They might be so if they pleased, but factions ran high, pretended patriots abused the peoples credulity, and —— I understand you, said she; your King is too good for them; they ought to have one that would make them fear him. If I was your Queen, I would soon curb their licentiousness; men cannot bear too much liberty.

After that, she enquired about the manners and dresses of our women, and I gave as faithful an account as was in my power, from my small acquaintance with polite company. She then

then faid, I perceive your nation is following exactly the fteps of all rich and powerful kingdoms; luxury has got in among you, and will foon deftroy you; but there is no ftability in this world, exclaimed fhe, with a figh!

She then concluded my audience, by faying, fhe fettled a penfion of two hundred tudorines yearly on me; and that fhe would likewife employ me in her fervice. But as fhe had been informed, that my countrymen had been in fearch of the fouthern continent, and that I wifhed to make a voyage to it; fhe would give directions to the Lurgow Amorow, not to appoint me to any fhip, till the feafon approached for the fleets failing to Luxo-volupto. In the mean time, continued fhe, I will appoint proper

proper persons to confer with you, on the different reformations which may be made in my navy, by the instructions it is in your power to give them. She then dismissed me, in great admiration of her good sense, and deep penetration; as well as much satisfied with her bounty, which prevented me from continuing a burthen to my friends. In weight of gold it was only equal to one hundred pounds English money; but in Ludorow would go as far as three times that sum in Britain.

The Drawing which I had learned, and very much practised for my amusement, became now of considerable use to me. The Lurgow Amorow being desirous to know, what were our ideas of beauty in the form of a ship, as well as what we reckoned beſt calculated for ſwift ſailing; with many other particulars, which no idea could be given of by deſcription; made me therefore endeavour to ſupply that defect by drawings.

I ſet to work then, and drew a ſhip of ſixty guns (which, in my opinion, was larger than any they were ſoon likely to have), from memory, in the beſt way I poſſibly could. She was repreſented in different appearances and ſituations; and therefore took up a good deal of time. The firſt was her hull, as complete, and lying in ordinary. The ſecond, a ſection of her. The third, when rigged. The fourth, under ſail. Figures with references to each part, were not omitted. And the fifth, were drawings of different parts and ornaments,

ments, which could not be fo well underſtood from their fmallnefs in the ſhip. Thefe were finiſhed as high as I poſſibly could, and prefented to the Lurgow Amorow; who was extremely well fatisfied with them; ordering them to be framed and glazed (after feveral copies had been taken, for the ufe of the furveyors of the Dock-Yards), and hung up in the Amoroutow Office as great curiofities. At a conference with the furveyors, I afterwards explained any difficulties they propofed to me, and gave them what farther lights my memory could fuggeſt.

My next meeting was with fome fea commanders, and aſtronomers, concerning the improvements made in England of the mariner's compafs and quadrant; as alfo what progrefs had

had been made in the difcovery of the longitude; the inftrument-makers being ordered to attend. Drawings were here alfo made ufe of; and after I had explained to them the advantages of ours, they readily acknowledged their fuperiority. I need fcarcely fay, that my quadrant was from the lateft improvements on Mr. Hadley's. I alfo acquainted them, that the needle did not always point to the north; and that to whatever caufe it was owing, the variation was conftantly changing (in every place of the ocean), fometimes in one direction, and fometimes in another. To find out that variation by the mean refult of feveral Azimuth compaffes, was what I next endeavoured to teach them; and had the fatisfaction to think they thoroughly underſtood me. I gave them alſo ſome little inſight into the theory of magnetiſm, with an account of the invention of artificial magnets, now only uſed, which appeared very ſurpriſing to them. My laſt attempt was to inform them of the progreſs which had been made, in the diſcovery of the longitude at ſea. I acquainted them with a premium, which had been offered by the Britiſh legiſlature, above half a century ago, of forty thouſand tudorines to any perſon who ſhould make a time-piece that would bear the motion of a ſhip, and the different degrees of heat and cold, in a voyage to a hot climate above a thouſand leagues diſtant, and back again, without varying above ſo much time from a good regulator, which was to be be kept on shore exactly true to time. That a mechanic of a wonderful natural genius, had spent in a manner his whole life upon it; and had brought it to such perfection, that (after having explained the whole mechanism to proper persons) he had received the premium. I told them, that one of these time-keepers was on board our ship, and was of great use to us. The other method of observing several distances of the sun and moon, with the way of working them, was also mentioned; together with the nautical almanac published by the King's astronomers, which saved a great deal of labour to the sea officers. The astronomers gave great attention to what I delivered, asked many questions for information, and wished to understand me;

me; but I thought it plain, that they were not yet sufficiently advanced in astronomy, to comprehend the principles on which it depended.

It is not to be supposed I could give their watch-makers any insight into the mechanism of the time-piece: but before we broke up, several compasses and quadrants were ordered to be made on my plan, and under my direction.

The third conference was held with the court physicians; in which I gave them an account of our victualling for the voyage, and especially that part of it, which experience had proved to be so efficacious in preventing the salted meat, which acquired some degree of putrefaction, from infecting the mass of blood; and causing that dreadful distemper,

so

so fatal to seamen in long voyages, the sea scurvy.

Our method also of keeping the men clean and the ship well aired, (was not forgot) by ventilators, windsails, and what was particularly used by the two ships in the last voyage, by fire.

In the next place, I acquainted them with the method of distilling sea-water, to make it fresh and useful for man, without having occasion to use more fire than was sufficient to dress the victuals of the ship's company.

I lastly gave them an account of another kind of distillation by cold, which our experience had furnished us, with, in the last voyage, that also freshened sea-water, and made it wholesome.

The

The Doctors were grave, senfible, candid men; they faid, the diftilling fea-water fhould be forthwith tried. And that my account of the fuccefs of the prefervatives from the fcurvy, had alfo fo much the appearance of truth, that they would certainly recommend the making trials of them, in the firft long voyages which occurred; as all the materials were fafe, and could have no bad confequences.

My laft conference was with Military men, of both fea and land fervice, with refpect to the improvement of their arms. That nation had known the ufe of gun-powder for a century paft, and had ufed cannon with fuccefs; but their fmall arms were ftill clumfy, with ill-contrived locks; and for that reafon few of them in their armies; pikes, and bows and arrows,

ftill

still continuing to be used. I could have wished now to have had my fusee with me for a pattern; but that not being to be had, I was obliged to make the best shift I could with drawings, and by the directions I gave the gun-smiths. The bayonet fixed to the muzzle of the piece, was also recommended as a much better weapon than the pike, and was acknowledged to be so. A musket and bayonet was made under my directions, and though clumsy, as the first attempt must of course be, both from my fault and the gun-smiths, was yet greatly admired by the officers; and by her Majesty's order many hands were set to work, to furnish the magazines with some thousands of them. Orders were also given to write to the merchants of Seripante, to endeavour

vour to recover my fufee from Uncomia at any price, as a more perfect model.

These were the principal improvements which I endeavoured to explain to them; but there were several others, which for brevity's fake are here omitted; fuch as the log-line, chain, pumps, the method of bending timber by fteam, &c. &c.

It was truly admirable to fee, with what candour every one of thefe worthy men behaved with regard to me; no little jealoufy or felf-intereft influenced them; but, with an open honefty, they acknowledged, after due examination, the fuperiority of our methods to their own. And feemed happy that Bonhommica had made fuch acquifitions by the accident of my coming among them; which might otherwife have taken centuries

to

to have found out, in the common course of things.

I afterwards found, that their reports to the ministers, had exactly answered what they had given me reason to expect. Her Majesty sent for me to court, and after graciously telling me how much her ministers were satisfied with the reports made by the different persons who had conferred with me, ordered me two hundred tudorines as a present to fit me out for my voyage to Luxo-volupto, which she said would not now be long of taking place.

I now became almost as great a favourite with the Lurgow Amorow and many of the other Lurgows, as I have been told my friend Omai was here.

I had

I had the honour to be invited frequently to dine and sup at their houses; where the entertainment was always plentiful, but the cookery simple and plain: no high seasoned ragouts, no made dishes appeared there. The wines were good, but drank in great moderation *.

There was always a proper mixture of the sexes at table, but great decorum kept up. The men, sensible and frank; the women, modest and reserved. No little scandal, or malicious reflections passed the women's lips, with respect to other women; but they, as well as the men, were very ready to speak of a commendable action done by any one. I shall

* The rule of not too much; by temperance taught,
In what thou eat'st, and drink'st; seeking from thence
Due nourishment, no gluttonous delight.
         Milton's Paradise Lost, Book xi. line 531.

mention some of that nature, which I heard talked of at different times; without any very extraordinary praise, but as things common enough.

A Physician who had attended a lady for a considerable time, ill of a distemper ; by the turn it took, plainly perceived he had mistaken the case; nature having relieved the patient in a way that could never have happened, if it had been as he supposed. Neither the lady, nor her friends, had any doubt but the salutary turn in her favour, was occasioned by the medicines he had prescribed. The physician however returned the fees he had received ; owning honestly, that he had been mistaken, and could not possibly retain money, he was conscious of having no right to.

Another

Another ſtill more extraordinary was, of an Attorney, who, by a miſtake, made by him in a writing, had loſt a client his law-ſuit. The client was not ſenſible on what the cauſe turned, nor in the leaſt blamed him; he honeſtly however paid him all that he had occaſioned the loſs of.

I ſhall mention but one more. A man had been left a conſiderable eſtate by a relation, on the preſumption that he was his neareſt of kin. The teſtator dying, he was put in poſſeſſion. Sometime after which he learned by accident, that there was one yet nearer to the deceaſed than himſelf; and being convinced it was the donor's intention to leave it to the heir at law, he ſent for him, honeſtly made a deed in his favour, and immediately reſigned it.

My being careffed by the Courtiers and Lurgows (or Nobility), did not however make me neglect my good friends the Merchants; or forget the worthy Ouragow, who recommended me to them. On the contrary, I paid them more attention than before, being fenfible that my prefent happy fituation was in a great meafure their work. When I got my penfion, my intention was to remove from Lurgofage's houfe to a lodging; that I might no longer be a burthen to him: but he would not hear of it, fo I ftill lived with him.

The fimplicity of manners that prevailed in Ludorow, was the caufe that there were no places of diffipation in that capital. No taverns, coffee-houfes, ball-rooms, concert-rooms, &c. &c.; but there was a theatre.

theatre. That indeed was but of a short standing; the size small, the decorations poor, and prices low.

I frequently went to it, and took notice, that the modesty and reserve of the sex, had prevented women from appearing on the scene; this to me, who had been accustomed to see women actresses in the theatres of England, had an unnatural appearance; but I soon became reconciled to it. Where men wear the ornament on their chins which nature has provided them with, a close shaved, smooth faced young man, who accustoms himself to imitate the behaviour of a woman, may be easily conceived to be one: and in my opinion, virtue and decency would have been much promoted in England, if that custom had still continued there.

For it muft be apparent to every body, that fcarcely one woman actrefs has appeared with any pretence to beauty, who has had the leaft regard to her character; nor been the lefs efteemed by the pnblic for that reafon. This has certainly had a bad effect on female manners, and made them look on crimes of that nature with lefs horror. But to return to the theatre of Ludorow.

The actors in general were far from contemptible, but they had few good dramatic poets. He who far furpaffed the reft, was an actor, and in that capacity, of very little merit: that was a reafon why his productions were lefs efteemed than they really deferved. I had been one evening to fee a new play of his, in company with Lurgofage and others of my friends. It went off extremely well, and I was charmed with it; however there were not wanting critics, who found fault with many parts; and which could not eafily be defended. One of thefe fupped with us at my friends, where the piece came naturally to be talked of; he loudly blamed the irregularity of the play; faid there was no plot, no contrivance, no moral; but juft a ftory taken from a novel, and put into dialogue; fhifting from place to place, and taking up years in the acting. All thefe objections are very juft, anfwered another; and certainly plays may be contrived more artfully; and to reprefent actions to our view with more probability. But that may be done merely by care and induftry, without the leaft fpark of genius:

genius: Avonfwan's excellency, is his knowledge of the human heart, and the paffions. Added to thofe, the moft poetical diction, and fineft flights of fancy; and I dare venture to prophecy, that when the man is no longer in view, and his profeffion become more honourable, that pofterity will do him juftice. I own my fentiments were exactly the fame, and genius fo feldom making its appearance, many things ought to be forgiven it when it does.

I was now informed by the Lurgow Amorow, that he had appointed me Carrogow (Poft Captain) to her Majefty's fhip Ardefow, of forty guns; under the Quadarow Moraveres: defiring me to call for my commiffion, and take the oaths required. He faid, she was to sail to Luxo-volupto as part of the convoy; that being necessary, (though the nation was in full peace), to prevent her Majesty's subjects, from being insulted by the Armoserian privateers.

I told him in answer, that my intentions were to serve so bountiful a Queen, and worthy a Nation, with all zeal and fidelity. But before I engaged myself, there were two conditions, which I earnestly wished might be granted me. He desired to know what they were; I replied, liberty of conscience in religion, and permission to depart, whenever an opportunity offered, to carry me to my own country. After a little consideration, he said, I ought to present a memorial to the Queen upon these subjects,

subjects, as he could not grant them, without an exprefs order from her. I followed the Lurgow Amorow's advice, and prefented one to this effect. Setting forth her Majefty's great goodnefs, in taking me into her fervice; which I embraced with the greateft joy, and fhould ferve her with all zeal and fidelity. But hoped her Majefty would have the goodnefs, to allow me liberty of confcience in religious matters. And having alfo a great love for my native country, and no chance of being conveyed thither, but by accidentally meeting at fea with an European fhip; that her Majefty would have the goodnefs to give orders, that if fuch an opportunity offered, I fhould have the liberty of departing, without incurring her difpleafure by fo doing.

She read my memorial directly, without referring it to her Minifters; and in anfwer to it faid, as to religion, every one in her kingdom enjoyed liberty of confcience; which fhe thought an abfolute effential to a free people. Befides, faid fhe, we all believe in the unity of the godhead as well as you chriftians. With refpect to the other part of it, I like you the better, continued fhe, for having an attachment to your native country, where your family and connections are: if you had not; how could I expect you would have any for me, or my people. I will not only give the orders defired, faid fhe; but if no opportunity fhould offer, I give you my royal word, that after having ferved me faithfully for feven years,

years, I will send a ship with you to the Cape of Good Hope, where I understand by your narrative, you may have frequent opportunities of returning to your own country; and no doubt you can easily conduct the vessel to that place. This filled me with such joy and gratitude, that I fell on my knees to thank her: she smiled, and graciously held out her hand for me to kiss. I went now and took the oaths; after which, my commission was given me, in which I was stiled Equihow or esquire. My next business was, to pay my respects to Moraveres, under whom I was to serve. He was the Quadarow or Commodore of this fleet, and was to carry a mark of distinction. He received me as well as I possibly could have desired; expressing the great satisfaction

faction he should have in conversing with me, on the manners and customs of my country; and especially in seeing the great improvements, which had been made by them in naval affairs, put by me into practice. I replied, that it was my great happiness to be appointed to serve under so great an officer, and worthy a man. That it would always give me infinite satisfaction to communicate any thing to him, that could in the least contribute to the good of the service. For that purpose I begged his permission to have the direction of fitting out the ship, and that the principal officers in each department, might have orders to furnish me with masts, sails, rigging, anchors, cables, &c. &c. according to the dimensions, and quality, I should demand. He answered,

wered, That it would give him great pleasure to see the Ardefow fitted out exactly in our manner; but having no power to order it of himself, all he could do, was to join me in making application to the Lurgow Amorow for an order to that purpose; and he had no doubt of our obtaining it. He judged right; when it was mentioned to that Minister, he said it was the very thing he had been thinking of; and all the necessary orders should immediately be given to that end; as well as for victualling her in the manner I had mentioned for a long voyage.

It may naturally be supposed that I did not fail to exert myself on this occasion; and fortunately I succeeded not only to my own satisfaction, but that of the ablest sailors in that country,

try. The ſhip was conſtantly filled with them; and I had numberleſs explanations to make; which (tho' often quite tired and vexed), I endeavoured to do with patience and temper. The fame of the Ardefows equipment extended itſelf; many of the Lurgows viſited her; and at laſt, a meſſage came to the Quadarow from the Lurgow Amorow, that her Majeſty would dine on board of her two days after. Great preparations were made for this entertainment, and as ſumptuous a one provided, as the time and place would admit. Her Majeſty came down the river in one of the royal barges, attended by ſeveral others full of courtiers of both ſexes; and on coming on board, was ſaluted by the Ardefow, and all the ſhips in the river. She then examined

the

the ſhip very narrowly, and had all the improvements explained to her; which ſhe almoſt as readily comprehended, as many of the ſea officers; expreſſing great ſatisfaction with the alterations which had been made. With the Quadarow's permiſſion, I reſolved to ſurpriſe her Majeſty and the court, with giving them a ſhort ſail on the river. The anchors were a-peak, and while they were at dinner, the ſails were ſet with as little noiſe as poſſible, without being in the leaſt perceived by the company. The firſt information they had of it, was the noiſe made by the rudder. Upon which, every body ran upon deck, and at laſt her Majeſty appeared there; who ſaid, laughing to me, that ſhe feared I was a dangerous traitor, ſince I had the boldneſs in
open

open day to carry off the Queen and Court; and she would have me punished for it. I answered her Majesty, that imagining she intended seeing every improvement which had been made, it was necessary to put the ship under sail for that purpose. We went only about a league down the river, and then returned to our former station. Soon after which the Queen and Court departed, seemingly very well satisfied with their entertainment.

Every thing being now ready for sailing, I went to court to take leave. Her Majesty said to me, I wish you a good voyage; take care of your morals among the Luxo-voluptans, and when you return, I will intrust you with a ship intirely under your own command. I took a most affectionate

tionate leave of my friends the Merchants, and left a letter for Ouragow to go with the fleet to Seripante.

We failed from the river Tourarow September 3d, 1775, with a fair wind. The convoy confifted of thirty-fix Merchant fhips, and there were two frigates of war, one of 28 guns, and another of 22, under the Quadarow's command. He left me the intire direction of the fhip, and was pleafed to fee, with what alertnefs I foon brought the crew to go through all their manœuvres.

Our courfe was weft quarter north. As nothing particular happened in the voyage, I fhall not trouble the reader with it. November 1ft, we made the land of Luxo-volupto early

in

in the morning: I heard them cry out land! land! and ran upon deck to view it, but could fee nothing but a blue cloud. I afterwards went up to the maft head, and ftill could fee nothing like the appearance of land. When I came down on the deck, and infifted they were miftaken; Moraveres fmiled, and faid, there was a peculiarity in the appearance of that land, which he never faw in any other; and it was by that means they always knew it. It puts on the appearance of a blue cloud, continued he, as if it wanted to conceal itfelf. Perhaps, purfued he, it is that which deceived Captains Cook and Furneaux your countrymen, and made them mifs it.

We came to an anchor with the whole fleet, in the harbour of Mirovolante,

volante, November 4th ; having been juſt two months and one day in our voyage.

CHAP. VI.

A Description of the Island of Bonhommica, and its Inhabitants. Their moral Sense. Manners, Customs, Laws, Government, Religion, &c. &c.

I SHALL now give as good an account of that Kingdom, as my short stay and best information will enable me. Bonhommica is an Island, lying betwixt 35° 46′ and 40° 35′ degrees of south latitude. And 165° 33′ and 170° 46′ east longitude. It is of an irregular shape, having many indentings of arms of the sea, and mouths of rivers, which form generally good harbours. It lies in a temperate climate, the southern hemisphere

phere being much colder in proportion to its latitude than the northern. A great part of it is naturally a good foil, fome diftricts however are mountainous and barren enough; but even thefe are fit for pafture. Inclofures are only to be feen near Ludorow, and the other great cities; the reft of the country is open. It produces very good corn, of moft of the kinds which we have in Europe; different forts of wines, olive oil, and many kinds of roots, greens, and fruits, which are cultivated in their gardens. Their animals are horfes, black cattle, fheep, goats, affes, fwine, and plenty of tame fowl. Befides their wild animals, which are deer, foxes, hares, wolves and bears, &c. They have many confiderable cities, amongft which,

Ludorow

Ludorow is the capital of the kingdom. It seems to be near one third as large as London, and stands on the banks of a beautiful navigable river; but it is far from being either handsome or magnificent. The streets are narrow, the houses of wood or brick, in a plain, but convenient enough stile of building. No magnificent churches, palaces, or squares adorn it; two of the churches indeed are large, and the royal palace, as well as severals belonging to the Lurgows, cover a great deal of ground, and have extensive gardens; but are all built in a stile of architecture, somewhat resembling what in Europe is called the gothic. The greatest beauty of that city in my opinion is, that you do not see a beggar; either occasioned by the virtue and industry

of

of the lower clafs of people, or by the private charities of the rich; for there is no poor-tax.

The inhabitants of Bonhommica are a well made, handfome people; very near as fair as the Englifh; moft commonly with blue eyes, but fometimes they are black or grey. Their hair, frequently of a reddifh colour, but more commonly black, chefnut, or flaxen. The hiftories of this country, make them of a very ancient eftablifhment in this Ifland, and even have fome fabulous accounts of their being a colony from fome far-diftant country; but on thefe, no dependence is to be made.

The drefs of the nobles, and better fort of gentry, is grave and decent; (refembling that of the Spaniards in

Philip II.'s time); the women covering up their arms and bosoms. It is made chiefly of woollen cloths or stuffs, manufactured by themselves. The nobility sometimes wear silks, or velvets, which they get from Luxovolupto; but no gold or silver are worn on the clothes of either sex, excepting on state days, when her Majesty is sometimes, for the greater magnificence, dressed in stuffs adorned with these metals.

Before I enter upon their manners, it will be previously necessary to mention a peculiarity in these people, which greatly influences them. It is, that they have six senses. The sixth sense, but which they reckon the first, is the sense of conscience, or the moral sense; and they would much rather

rather be without any of the others, even the fight or hearing, than destitute of it. There are certainly some glimmerings of this sense, in other nations, but they are so slight, that they have been almost intirely overlooked. But in this people it is so apparent, that no doubt can be made of it. It is true they take a great deal of pains to cultivate it in their children, from their earliest infancy; arguing, that as we may strengthen our limbs or other senses by using them; so we may this sense, by constantly habituating them to the practise of it. To that end, the first eight or ten years of their education, (except in learning to read their own language, writing, arithmetic, and geography), is employed by their parents and masters in improving and fortify-

ing them in the use of that excellent sense. Their method of doing this, is chiefly by examples from their own history, and short stories written of virtuous actions, done by their countrymen or country-women. I need not say, that the sex makes no difference in this part of education; though after a certain age, it is carried on separately. The examinations which they go through, are not on a part of speech in a dead language; but to give their opinions in doubtful actions, whether they are blameable or praise-worthy; putting questions to them, how they would act in such and such situations, and rectifying their judgments if necessary. The good example shewed by all around them, has likewise no small influence. Rewards and punish-
ments

ments are also used with great propriety; being certain badges of approbation or shame, worn for a certain time according to the merit or demerit of the wearer. Preventive methods are no less carefully attended to. They can meet with no improper books, as none such are published; and every word or action which shews a tendency to the depravation of the heart, is carefully watched and checked at its first appearance. To all these, the precepts of their religion are superadded, which shall be taken notice of in its proper place. During all this time, innocent amusements and diversions, are rather encouraged than otherwise; being looked on by them, as salutary both to the body and mind.

The

The females are educated intirely under the maternal eye, who, from their retired way of life, have fufficient time, and take a pleafure in cultivating their young minds, and training them up, in all the virtues proper for their fex and ftation. Boarding fchools for girls are not known in that country; where one or two vicious characters are fufficient to corrupt the whole.

When the boys are fourteen or fifteen, they are fent to the Cadorow, or the univerfity ; where they are carefully inftructed in the learning which is in vogue in this country; having ftill a watchful eye to the ftrengthening and improving the moral fenfe : that learning chiefly confifts in explaining the phyfics,

meta-

metaphyfics, logic, and other writings of an old author, called Ariftorow, whom they look on as infallible; and he who underftands him beft, is deemed the moft learned. They have not yet begun to think for themfelves, and to inveftigate truth by reafoning and experiments.

From this, it will be concluded, that the ftate of learning is low among them; it certainly is fo, in comparrifon with England. Some Poets they have; but none deferving the name of an Hiftorian. Of Mathematics, Geometry, Natural and Experimental Philofophy, Aftronomy, Anatomy, Chymiftry, Phyfics, and Natural Hiftory, they know but very little. The theory of Gravitation, by which the great Newton has explained all

all the motions of the Planets and even of the Comets, they are intirely ignorant of; as well as of the later difcovery of Electricity, which has brought fo many wonders to light. The Moral fenfe is what they are chiefly to be valued for; and furely in the fcale of human happinefs, it vaftly outweighs all our boafted acquifitions*.

Their language is rough, but copious; refembling, in its found and the character they ufe, the German more than any other European tongue.

Writing they have been poffeffed of, for many centuries; but printing

---

* One moral, or a mere well natured deed,
Can all defert in fciences exceed.
    Duke of Buckingham to Mr. Pope,
    Pope's Works. Vol. I.

is only a late difcovery: which probably will diffufe knowledge among them, as it has done in Europe; but whether to their advantage or the contrary, is hard to determine.

The Bonhommicans are a brave, generous, and virtuous people; but their courage is only fhewn in ferving their country, and their virtue does not make them morofe or felf-fufficient. They are ftrongly attached to liberty, and great œconomifts, both to preferve themfelves independant, and be able to affift the neceffitous. The Lurgows are much refpected, which they take care to preferve by their manner of living; but fuperior virtues or abilities are much more fo. A virtuous man is not defpifed becaufe he is poor, nor a rich man refpected

refpected merely becaufe he is fuch, without any other recommendation.

The men are generally chearful in converfation, but feldom lively, volatile, or giddy. In mixed companies, a modeft referve is the character of their women; but in their own houfes, among their relations, that is laid afide, and they are lively and agreeable.

The occupations of each man's different profeffion employs his time; he fpends none of it idly in drunkennefs and debauchery, but returns home to his wife, whom he is fure to find attending to her domeftic cares. Not but they entertain one another fometimes, and go to fee a play; but that happens but feldom, and does not deferve mentioning.

The

The Lurgows who have not places at court, reside constantly upon their estates in the country; where they keep open house for all their neighbours, serving them with their friendship and advice in the country, and their interest if necessary at court.

Their wives generally employ themselves, in the midst of a number of young women of small fortunes, on some great piece of needle-work for furniture; which, with music and visiting, fills up their time very agreeably.

Games like chess and draughts, I have seen played at; but they know nothing of cards or dice, nor any kind of gaming for money.

The only conveyance known (till lately) in that country for all ranks
of

of people, is riding on horfeback. Some few coaches have been within thefe few years introduced from Luxovolupto; of which her Majefty, and fome of the firft nobility, are the only poffeffors.

In their dealings and intercourfe betwixt man and man, they are perfectly upright; and fo far from taking an advantage of another, that if they find they have made a miftake to their own benefit, they are never eafy in their minds till it is rectified. Some inftances of this are given in the former chapter.

They are alfo punctual obfervers of their promifes, and conftant in their friendfhips.

Polygamy is not allowed of among them, but divorces are on three accounts, (though feldom ufed but for
the

the laſt), unfaithfulneſs, diſagreement of tempers, and barrenneſs. Upon proofs of any one of theſe it is eaſily obtained, but care is taken that the children do not ſuffer. The women have the ſame right as the men; but the children always fall to the latter's care.

To prevent marriages being made from motives of intereſt and not from affection, the laws do not allow women to be capable of inheritance; but when their parents die, they are left an annuity ſufficient to ſupport them in the rank they had hitherto lived in; which upon their marriage devolves to the head of the family. If they are divorced, the huſband is obliged to allow them the annuity again, or a greater, if he is of a higher rank than her father was.

The men frequently marry in a rank beneath them, as it does not degrade their family; but the women feldom or never do.

Duty and refpect to parents, are juftly carried to a great degree of veneration while they live; and when they die, they do not make ufe of an undertaker to put them in the ground, and perhaps fend them out of their houfes, as foon as their fouls have departed. But all thofe (whom affliction has not rendered incapable) attend them to the grave, with true heart-felt forrow, but no affected noify exclamations of it. The place where their bodies are laid, is frequently vifited by them, to call back to their remembrance, the many benefits, and wife inftructions, they had received from the authors (under God)

God) of their being, and to fortify them in virtue.

Their government is a limited monarchy, like ours in Britain; confifting of a King (or Queen), Lurgows, or houfe of Lords, and delegates from the people called houfe of Burgows. The prerogative of the crown is great, and the claims of the people very extenfive; yet they live in a perfect good underftanding. The Queen has entirely gained the confidence of her fubjects, from her prudent œconomy and wife meafures of government; never afking money of her people, but when their fafety and happinefs makes it abfolutely neceffary.

The members of both houfes have opportunities of fhewing their parts and oratorial abilities as in ours; but the moral fenfe has one bad effect on thefe occafions; it confines them to their real fentiments upon the fubject they are fpeaking on, and confequently fhortens very much their fpeeches, and cramps their genius.

Another very great obftruction to the formation of great orators in this country, is, there being no oppofition to the court; by which the members might (if they were capable of ufing fuch means) force themfelves into places, by their talents of harangueing; either for, or againft the meafures in queftion. This leaves to her Majefty the full exertion of her great judgment, in filling places with the perfons moft capable of well executing them.

The

The delegates for the houfe of Burgows are chofe with great quietnefs and decency; no candidates appear to canvas the electors ; no houfes are open to treat them with victuals and liquor, and make them neglect their bufinefs for weeks together. The principal confideration of the electors is to find out, who are the moft virtuous men among them ; and of thofe which can beft be fpared from their avocations. When they have fixed on the perfon, a deputation is fent to him, begging he will take the trouble of reprefenting the county or borough in the Witterow: the expence of which will be bore by them. If he undertakes it, they go in a body and return him thanks ; if otherwife, they fix on fomebody elfe, until fuch time as one accepts.

Salaries are annexed to all places under government, in proportion to their dignity and truſt; but all very low in compariſon with ours in England; the public money being carefully huſbanded. But that does not prevent their being accepted of by the worthieſt men, as they believe it an honour as well as a duty to ſerve their country. And it is a very common thing for the Lurgows and rich Burgows, to decline the acceptance of their ſalaries; ſaying, there was no merit in ſerving for hire, and that it was a ſhame for thoſe who could live in ſplendour without it, to prey upon their country.

Sine-cure places are not known in Bonhommica; nor are perquiſites of any kind allowed to be taken, in any of the public offices: but buſineſs is
carried

carried on (to my own knowledge in moſt of them) with great civility, accuracy, and difpatch.

The taxes are very low, confiſting of about two-pence in the pound on the rent of land; and duties on articles of Merchandife imported, and on fome exports. Thefe duties are collected at a very fmall expence, as the Merchants are very punctual in paying their duties at the proper offices without being called on: and fcarcely one inſtance is known of an attempt to defraud the government by fmuggling; it being looked upon as a kind of facrilege againſt their country.

Bonhommica, befides its coaſting trade, which breeds a great number of good failors, has a pretty confiderable

able foreign one. They have factories at Miro-volante, Seripante, and some other places; and the first named city has one at Ludorow, from a member of which, I had some instructions in the Luxo-voluptan language. Their exports are fine and coarse cloths of their own manufacture, corn of different kinds, wine, oil, houshold furniture, &c. &c. Imports are silks, velvets, linen cloths, cotton ditto; wines of higher flavour, spices, porcelane, curious pieces of workmanship in gold or silver, pictures, statutes, &c. from Luxo-volupto; wool &c. as mentioned before, from Auditante, and other commodities too tedious to mention, from these and other places. On the whole, I learned from good hands, that the balance was

was confiderably in favour of Bonhommica.

A ftanding army is not kept up in this country, in time of peace; as in their opinion it would be dangerous to liberty, withdrawing a number of hands from the national induftry; and from the idlenefs in which foldiers generally pafs their time, when not employed in warlike operations, might be dangerous to their virtue.

In place of that, they have an excellent Militia of 40,000 men, who are carefully difciplined for three weeks, twice a year; and have arms and cloathing lodged for them in the hall of each county town, to be ready on any emergency.

I am perfuaded very great dependence may be placed on this Militia.
Officers

Officers and Men whofe breafts are animated with the love of their country, at the fame time that their bodies are healthy and vigorous, from habits of fobriety and induftry would be very formidable to any invaders. But except it were to affift a people whofe liberties were oppreffed, I queftion whether they could be brought to leave their country, and act offenfively upon fuch quarrels as our European wars are commonly grounded.

Their arms are bows and pikes, with fome few clumfy mufkets, as has been already mentioned.

Having had the ufe of great guns for a confiderable time, a regiment of artillery is conftantly kept up, and a fmall corps of engineers.

Her

Her Majefty's great penetration having difcovered to her, that the beft defence of an Ifland was a powerful navy, has laboured for fome years to create (as I may term it) a maritime force, and not without fuccefs. She has already got between thirty and forty fhips of war of all fizes; the largeft of which indeed, does not equal one of our fhips of fifty guns; but that is a great deal for the time; and as her fubjects make excellent failors, I have no doubt but in a century or two (if the fame wife meafures are purfued) that kingdom will become a great maritime power. Happy am I in the reflection, that it has been my good fortune, to contribute in fome fmall degree to the attaining of fuch wife purpofes. So great

great a Princefs, and fuch virtuous fubjects, deferve the affiftance of God and Man.

The Queen, though unguarded, (but by a few halberdiers, more for fhow than ufe), is fafe in the affections of her people. Her court, without being adorned with jewels, or the precious metals, derives a great luftre from the characters of all who belong to it. She affects pomp and fhow, from her knowledge of their effects on the minds of men, but takes care they do not coft more than they are worth, being perfect miftrefs of the uncommon talent, of uniting œconomy with dignity.

The principal officers of her houfehold, and ladies of her bed-chamber, are generally above receiving their
falaries;

salaries; but neverthelefs are punctual in their attendance, and have the honour of eating at her Majefty's table. One is kept for the maids of honour, who in other refpects think themfelves fufficiently honoured by their appointment; her Majefty being very careful in her choice of thefe young women, and confequently they are fure of marrying well.

Her Majefty has no fixed days, and hours, for receiving thofe of her fubjects, who are intitled by their rank to appear at court. She lives at her palace like the mother of a great family; feeing them at all hours: at her rifing, and going to bed, as well as at other times. And once a week when the court is in Ludorow, fhe dines in public, when all ranks and

degrees

degrees are admitted into the galleries which overlook the saloon. These things certainly help to make her popular, though it may be thought a great constraint, and very disagreeable to live always in public. She knows however very well when to be alone, or with a particular society; and has such an authoritative manner, that the least hint or nod is observed and obeyed. Sometimes balls are given at court, when they dance according to their fashion, which is graceful enough. Masks are also exhibited, and sometimes tragedies and comedies in the theatre of the palace. But her Majesty sees them more frequently at the public one, mixing with all ranks of her people in their amusements, where she is received with great acclamations.

They have an entertainment which is only given at court on extraordinary occasions; such as the visit of some great foreign prince, whom they intend doing honour to. It is of a military nature, somewhat resembling the tilts and tournaments we read of in former times. The Bonhommicans are very expert at it, and generally use the Auditantine horses on these occasions, as they are handsomer and more docile than their own. One of them was held when I was at Ludorow, in honour of prince Anjouvini, who came from another large Island to propose marriage to her Majesty. She paid him great honours, and as it suited her politics, even gave him some encouragement,

but

but concluded nothing. The Prince penetrating her defigns, took leave, and returned to his own country.

It may be perceived from what has been faid, that money is not a principal object with this virtuous nation; but they are greatly ambitious of being diftinguifhed by their fovereign, and proud of being employed by her. To be raifed to the rank of Lurgow, or from a lower to a higher rank in that line, is not indifferent to them; and the wearing a certain garter for life is much coveted. There are but few who have the latter privilege, and their number is always kept full. But the Lurgowfhip is entirely in her Majefty's power, to create as many as fhe pleafes: this however fhe is very fparing of, the better to keep up its value.

Never was there a civilised nation on earth, which had so little occasion for laws as this I am now writing of, because they are a law unto themselves; but none can do absolutely without them. The laws of Bonhommica are wise, plain, and few; their whole code being comprised in a small octavo volume. They do not think those laws can be good, which are always requiring alteration or amendment. Sometimes, however, the Witterow find it necessary, from the vicissitude of human affairs, to make new ones; but that seldom happens. An excellent preliminary one is, that no suit shall be above a month before any court until it is determined. The judges are made independent of the crown as in England; but in comparison with ours, their places are perfect fine-cures. When any cafe of property, of too great intricacy to be unravelled by the moral fenfe, falls out; the parties refer it to three of the wifeft of their neighbours, whom they empower to take the opinions of counfel at their joint expence, and oblige themfelves to abide by the determination of thefe umpires. But fhould it happen, that from the tendernefs of their confciences, they are prevented from coming to a decifion, it is then amicably fubmitted to a judge and jury. Though they have a right to appeal to the houfe of Lurgows, it is very feldom carried fo far.

It will readily be perceived, that the Law here is not near fo lucrative a profeffion as in England; nor is there

there a tenth part of the number of its profeſſors. The counſellors live in hopes of being judges, and the attorneys by writing deeds, contracts, &c. &c.

In their criminal law, death is only inflicted on thoſe who are guilty of the moſt atrocious offences; and then it is executed with great ſolemnity, attended with all the circumſtances which can move the ſpectators with horror, without cruelty to the ſufferer. For ſmaller crimes, hard labour for a certain term is the uſual puniſhment; but if they ſeem incorrigible (to prevent their corrupting others), they are baniſhed to Luxovolupto, where they paſs very well.

There had not been a capital puniſhment in the whole kingdom,

during

during the reign of her prefent Majefty, which had lafted betwixt fixteen and feventeen years; and while I was in Ludorow there was none of any kind, excepting one poor woman, who was led about the ftreets with a paper on her breaft for being given to lying.

The religion of this country, or to fpeak more properly, the Seraphite religion (for it is not profeffed here only, but in Luxo-volupto and other countries), feems to me, of all the falfe ones which have got footing in the world, to be the beft; for I can give no faith to its pretended divine original. The tradition they have concerning its founder, is as follows:

That eight enturies ago, Serapha (a native of the ifland of Bonemolo, 500 leagues

500 leagues from Bonhommica) lying one night awake in his bed, saw a beautiful apparition in a human form, whose whole person was illumined, and spoke to him thus,—Serapha you are a good man, and I have chose you to reform your countrymen, and the rest of the world, from idolatry, and the other crimes they are in constant practice of. Go then and inform them what you have seen, and that it is my command they no longer worship idols made by their own hands, but that great power which made and sustains all things. That the worship they pay, should be a spiritual one, adoring his power and goodness, praying for his constant protection, and thanking him for benefits received. Let them know that their souls are immortal, and

according to their lives here, will their ſtate in a future life be happy or miſerable. When you have made ſome progreſs in your miſſion, I will again ſee you, and give more particular directions concerning their behaviour to one another. Seraphа remained in the greateſt awe and ſurpriſe for ſome time after it diſappeared; he conſidered with himſelf, whether it was not a dream, and being convinced that he had been awake the whole time, believed it was ſomething ſupernatural, and ought to be obeyed.

Next day, he acquainted his friends with the meſſage he had orders to deliver; ſome made a jeſt of it, but others were ſtruck with the ſublimity of the doctrine. It gained ground by by degrees, so that the whole inhabitants of Bonemolo in a short time destroyed their idols, and left off many of their crimes.

Two years and three months after its first appearance, Serapha had another visit from the apparition, in the night also when lying in bed. It said to him, he had done well, that his countrymen had broke their idols to pieces, and seemed to be in a disposition to make a thorough reformation in their lives; to assist them in which, he had brought him, according to his promise, a directory or guide, by which they ought to conduct themselves, if they valued their own happiness either in this world or the next. He then gave Serapha a book, and desired him to

be

be active in spreading the benefits it contained, for that he should see him no more, upon which he vanished from his sight.

Serapha immediately arose, and struck a light, to examine the book; which was wrapped in a mantle of fine stuff, the like of which had never been seen in that island. The writing was in the Bonemolo language, but so exquisitely performed, that no body could come any thing near imitating its beauty, when many copies were at first taken. That original writing is lodged in the chief temple of Bonemolo, and is held in the highest reverence. Many translations have been made of it into different languages; and it is called the Serephatic (or holy book). I read a great a great part of it, and acknowledge it to be a very good fyftem of morality; inferior only to our gofpel in the perfection of its doctrines. This Religion fpread over many countries, when Serapha, grown old and in high veneration, fuddenly difappeared, and was never heard of more. The followers of his religion concluded he was taken from among them alive, into the divine abode, where good men were to be rewarded; but pay no worfhip to him, nor to the apparition, for which they have no other name, as it never explained itfelf to Serapha on that head.

The difappearing of Serapha, is the Æra from which they begin to compute their time.

I never heard of any famous difciples or followers that he had, or of any sects formed amongst them.

Their temples are some of them large, but unadorned; no statues or pictures being allowed of in them.

The worship is simple, consisting of prayers in general terms, and sometimes in seasons of distress for particular benefits; and thanksgivings for constant support and protection.

One day in the week is appointed for that purpose, but they have no holydays.

Their clergy is held in great esteem, and their pious and exemplary lives truly intitle them to it. They have however neither wealth nor power, but are supported in a decent mediocrity

ocrity by the ſtate, and are diſmiſſible from their functions at pleaſure by the crown; but of that there is no inſtance remembered.

As there is no hierarchy, and conſequently no dignitaries, &c. the prieſts are few, being only one to each pariſh, and ſometimes two, when it happens to be very extenſive. Viſitation of the ſick is a duty moſt conſcientiouſly performed by them; but I never heard of, or ſaw any preaching. Probably they think it unneceſſary, as what they are to believe concerning the unity, wiſdom, power, juſtice, &c. &c. of the deity is ſo very plain; the moral ſenſe ſupplying alſo ſo well what is required of them to their neighbour. I ſhall conclude this chapter with obſerving, that

that their temples on days of worſhip are amazingly crouded ; and the whole congregation ſeem actuated with a fervor of devotion and adoration, truly worthy of this virtuous people.

CHAP.

CHAP. VII.

The Commanders of the Ships of War invited to ly at the Merchants houses of the Bonhommican Factory at Mirovolante. Of the pretended superiority of the Luxo-voluptans in the Sense of Taste. Commonness of Wheel Carriages in Miro-volante. A wonderful stigma on failures in chastity in both sexes. Sees Garramond a famous Actor in one of Avonswan's Plays. The Commanders introduced at Court. The Author sought after by the Nobility, as coming from a far country. Balls, Routs, Concerts. A Masquerade. Maraveres taken ill. Practice of Physic. State of Luxo-volupto, and neighbouring Kingdoms. The Bonhommican sailors mobbed on a rejoicing night, for the election of a Patriot.

I NOW return to the harbour of Miro-volante, where the fleet was

left

left at an anchor. It lies in 38° 15' fouth latitude, and in 132° 24' weft longitude. I was very much and agreeably ftruck, with the appearance of this city from the water. The amazing extent of it, the fuperb domes, lofty fpires, grand columns, magnificent palaces, &c. &c. all built in a light, airy, but pleafing architecture, of a perfectly new tafte, made it feem worthy to be the capital of the world.

Several Merchants of the factory foon came on board, to congratulate us on our fafe arrival; and with fuch honeft earneftnefs preffed the Quadarow and the other Commanders, to take beds at their houfes, that there was no refufing them. Moraveres was engaged to Moragow, the Commanders of the frigates to two others,

and

and myself to Nicophange. We went ashore with them to that quarter of the town where the Merchants lived for the conveniency of their commerce, called the city.

We dined that day with Morogow, where I was very much surprised to see a table set out with all the elegance and magnificence that could be well conceived, far surpassing any thing I had seen among the first nobility at Ludorow. After dinner, when we were drinking a sober glass of delicious wine, Moragow said to me (for Moraveres and the others had been there before), I observed your surprise at dinner, to see us Merchants live in so different a style from what is customary in Bonhommica, but I assure you it is not from choice but necessity. For as we are obliged to

have

have great connections with the Miro-volante Merchants, and to have them at our tables both by invitation and accidentally, we are obliged to comply with their manners. Besides, said he, if we did not, we could get no Luxo-voluptan servants to live with us, and we could not well do without some of them. I asked him, if he could account for that very great difference in the way of living, that was observable in these two nations. He answered, that the Luxo-voluptans pretended their sense of taste, or palate, was naturally formed more sensible of agreeable impressions than other nations. That even their philosophers were of that opinion, but for his part he believed it a vitiated taste, become from long habit a kind of second nature. From their extenfive

five dominions in the southern hemisphere, continued he, and immense commerce, they had it in their power to indulge that vitiated taste, by ransacking half the globe for choice viands, the finest flavoured wines, and the most poignant sauces to gratify their appetite. But what will very much surprise you still continued he, is, that the meanest servant-maid in Miro-volante, must breakfast on the infusion of an herb, that is brought ten thousand leagues from this country, with the produce of a cane to sweeten it, which also comes from a great distance. I believe, said I in reply, That must be what we call in Britain Tea, and is brought from China. Their name for it, said he, is Cha, and probably is brought from the same country, to which they send many ſhips yearly, to a port called Nanking. This ſhewed me the reaſon, why the Engliſh ſhips had never met any of theirs.

The difcourfe ftill continuing on their luxurious way of life, one of the company mentioned the great diſtance from which they brought an amphibious ſhell-animal alive (ſometimes of immenſe ſize), which was one of their greateſt regales. They drefs it up in a rich wine, with many warm fpices, faid he, devouring it in fuch quantities, that they have loofe dreſſes made on purpofe for theſe feaſts, their uſual garments confining them too much. I plainly faw they meant turtle; but out of regard to my own dear country, took no notice of the ſame beaſtly cuſtom prevailing in it.

It

It occurred to me however to aſk, if that way of life did not prejudice their healths. Very much, ſaid Nicophange; it brings on the gout, and many other painful and lingering diſorders, which make their lives miſerable *; but that neither deters others, nor (ſuch is their propenſity to theſe poiſons) even the ſufferers themſelves from again indulging in them, as ſoon as the weakly and almoſt deſtroyed tone of their ſtomachs will permit. A rare country for phyſicians, cried I! That it is, ſaid Moragow, and we abound with them. Beſides the regular bred ones, there are alſo irregulars in great numbers with their noſtrums; and twenty quack medicines ſold in book-

* While they pervert pure nature's healthful rules
To loathſome ſickneſs.
    Milton's Paradiſe Loſt, Book xi. line 523.

ſellers

sellers shops as infallible remedies for every disease the human body is subject to. These we may reasonably conclude do much more harm than good; but a few real or fictitious cures well puffed in the news-papers, make the fortune of the proprietor of a medicine; as bold assertions have great weight with this credulous people, and none who have suffered by the use of it, are virtuous enough, or at least will give themselves the trouble to warn mankind against its pernicious effects.

It would be tedious to give the reader the whole conversation which passed, concerning this extraordinary people; but it seemed to be the unanimous opinion of the Bonhommicans, that whether their exquisite sense of taste was natural or acquired, there was scarcely a vestige of the moral sense left among the generality of them, though there were indeed many and great exceptions.

We were to dine next day at Nicophange's, who, after he had done his material business, kindly offered to walk with me to view the city. The streets were extremely crouded with people, and one would have thought all the coaches in the universe were assembled in this capital. Seeing Nicophange frequently saluted from them, I took the liberty of asking him what great men they were (hoping he would excuse the curiosity of a stranger). He very civilly desired me to ask any questions I thought proper, as things occurred, while we continued our walk. The first that afterwards faluted him, he told me was a Merchant; No doubt extremely rich, faid I. That is very doubtful, replied he; it is very common here, to make the moſt ſhow when there is the leaſt fubſtance. The next, who made him a low bow from his carriage, he told me, was the Phyſician whom he employed: No doubt, faid I, he makes a great deal by his practice, as he keeps his coach. He is, anſwered he, a very learned, and honeſt man; but know, that in this vaſt city, the phyſicians who have but three or four patients in different parts of the town, cannot poſſibly attend them on foot; befides, going into houſes where perhaps they never were before, with their ſhoes all covered over with dirt, would be very indelicate. The third, he faid, was his Taylor: Is there

there a neceffity for his riding in a carriage alfo, faid I? He laughed, and anfwered no; but that he had the ambition to be employed by the Nomras (grandees), though it probably would be his ruin, as their extravagance often put it out of their power (if they had the inclination) to pay their debts, and it was very difficult to compel them to it. In fhort, there were Apothecaries, Players, Dancing and Singing mafters, Tooth-drawers, and Corn-cutters; and many other ftill lower trades in other parts of the world, all figuring away in their carriages; fo that all ranks and degrees of life feemed to be confounded. While at the fame time there were fuch numbers of beggars peftering every body who walked, that I could not tell what to make of such a medley.

Perhaps, if I had known the capital of my own country a little better, my surprise would not have been so great.

At dinner I was introduced to the acquaintance of a Luxo-voluptan by Nicophange; he was called Bonaris, and from a similarity of character was fond of Bonhommican company. I happened to sit next him at table, and found him very polite and communicative. When we broke up from dinner, he said to me, As you are the greatest stranger to the manners and customs of this country, I shall be very happy in giving you any information in my power, and shall be ready to attend you to places of curiosity or amusement; while at the same time I hope you

you will not refuse me the favour of informing me sometimes of particulars concerning yours. I am, continued he, an idle man; my fortune is independent, and I have no family cares, being unmarried; my time is paſſed in rational amuſements, or literary purſuits, ſometimes in town, and ſometimes in the country, juſt as I am in the humour. You ſee then that my attendance on you, will not break in on any of my more important affairs, and is therefore no kind of compliment, but doing myſelf a pleaſure. I anſwered him in the ſame frank manner, and we agreed to go directly to the public walks.

It being a fine evening, there was a great deal of what is called good company. The women in general
ſeemed

seemed handsome, but one particularity of theirs drew very much my attention; they appeared to have wings on their heads. Good God! said I, to Bonaris; have the women wings in this country? Those on the womens heads, are of little importance, replied he with a smile, but many of both sexes have others of the greatest consequence, and from a cause which you cannot possibly form any idea of; to add to your wonder, let me inform you, that we were not always thus stigmatized by them, but have had the honour of meriting this distinction, by an unbounded indulgence in voluptuousness. I begged him to explain himself, which he said he would do, but first desired me to take notice of the shape of many persons, both men and women.

After

After having confidered them with fome attention, I told him the only thing particular I obferved, was an uncommon fullnefs about many of their fhoulders. That is fufficient, faid he, and I fhall now proceed to fatisfy your curiofity (after having premifed, that what I have to fay is fo very extraordinary, if you fhould ever have an opportunity of relating it to your countrymen, they would probably fuppofe this prodigy to be only Immodefty allegorized; but you will foon be convinced of its being ftrictly true).

Befides the acutenefs of our fenfe of Tafte, faid he, which you muft have heard of, we have alfo that of Touch or Feeling in as exquifite a degree as human nature is capable of fupporting;

porting, without turning pleasure into pain; especially in the commerce betwixt the sexes †. This however produced no bad effects, whilst our manners continued plain and modest. But about a century ago, when they became very loose, from the bad example of one of our Kings, a very surprising phenomenon made its appearance, the cause of which has never been accounted for in a natural way, by our greatest Philosophers, and must therefore be deemed supernatural. It is most probably meant to expose the vice, by setting a mark upon the guilty; for though they assist them in committing it, that they were given for that purpose, I think

---

† But if the sense of touch, whereby mankind
Is propagated, seem such dear delight
Beyond all other.
        Milton's Paradise Lost, Book viii. line 579.

cannot

cannot be fuppofed. This phenomenon is a pair of wings fprouting from every woman's fhoulders, immediately after a failure in chaftity; and from every man's, who has feduced a young maiden, or married woman. As thefe are repeated, or ‡ according to the ftrength of their defires, the wings increafe in fize, till they become in full proportion to the body; and if the vice is left off from a fincere repentance, they gradually decreafe till they entirely vanifh. You fee both men and women endeavour to hide them under their clothes, but it is in vain, unlefs they are very fmall indeed. But they ufe them with great fpirit to carry them to an

‡ Methinks I feel new ftrength within me rife,
Wings growing.
   Milton's Parabife Loft, Book x. line 243.
[Speech of Sin, after Eve was feduced.]

affigna-

affignation. Thofe women who have loft all fhame, and wear them publicly, are called Alæ-putas; Women of fafhion, often more inexcufable than the others, only Galanteras; and the other fex, by far the moft blameable of all, Corrumperos.

As to thofe on the women's heads, it is only a fign of diffipation, or violent paffion for public places; but it is generally obferved, that thofe whofe wings on that place are unufually high, foon have them appear on their fhoulders, which the men call being fledged. One thing more I muft mention, which is, that many Nomrinas (women of quality) though very well provided, are fo lazy, as not even to ufe them to meet their lovers; but have little Cars provided, to which they harnefs Pigeons, Cuckows,

kows, Pheafants, or other birds, which they fecretly keep for that purpofe. In this they are followed by the Alæ-putas in greateſt vogue, by way of giving themfelves airs. For generally they are not content with becoming imitators, but give the ton to moſt parts of female drefs; the fex wifely confidering, that as it is the fole ſtudy of thefe Nymphs to allure the men, they muſt be the beſt judges of what will pleafe them. I have even heard of fome men who were guilty of that piece of effeminacy. As they ufe their wings in fome meafure at the fame time, very flight efforts are neceffary from the birds. This phenomenon furprifed me more than even the Taupinierans had done, and while he yet fpoke, it occurred to me, that a ſtigma on

the

the guilty perfon was more juft than our notions in Europe, of fixing an ideal pair of horns on the forehead of the poor hufband.

When Bonaris had ended, I obferved to him, that in my country, Cupid, or the paffion of love, was always allegorically reprefented with wings, that the ardency of an amorous flame was metaphorically called winged in poetry, and a learned Bifhop had attempted to invent artificial wings for mankind; but I never expected to meet with a People, where the votaries of love fhould be equipped with adventitious ones. I had fcarcely faid thefe words, when we faw two very fine women coming towards us, with their wings difplayed; O the angels, exclaimed I! for they brought
pictures

pictures of these divine beings into my mind. If they are Angels, replied he laughing, they are fallen ones, and I would advise you to have nothing to say to them, or you may probably repent it. So thought I to myself, then they have got that cursed bane to love, even into this country; but how should it be brought? that subject however took up little of my attention, as my thoughts were so full of the other. Do not these wings, said I, occasion a great many divorces, as they are a sure proof of incontinency? Many jealousies, replied he; but as by our laws they are no proof, and divorces can only be obtained in this country for adultery, it rather enables them to avoid being detected, by making their assignations so much the easier. On observing the heads of the women, and finding them almoſt all alike; I remarked to my friend, that the females of Mirovolante muſt in general have a great paſſion for diſſipation, as they all had wings on their heads. There, ſaid he, you are deceived; the caſe is this. The winged ones being the ton, have made their feathers appear ſo elegant by their manner of ſhaping, ſtaining, and dreſſing them, that they are become ſo much the faſhion; that all other women of any genteel ſtation are obliged to imitate them, and wear falſe ones.

It now grew dark, and we retired from the walks. In our way to the Merchants quarter, we went through a ſtreet where there were great numbers of Alæ-putas taking little ſhort flights, and hopping about with

Hild Bowman delin.t & Sculp.t See Page

with defign to engage their prey. While I was in ferious difcourfe with my friend on the neglect or connivance of the magiftrates, in fuffering fuch nuifances, whereby the temptations of a brothel were brought into the public ftreets; expofing unwary youth when going about their neceffary affairs, to be feduced into vice and difeafe; efpecially as Bonaris faid, that houfes of entertainment were every where open for the reception of thefe nymphs and their paramours for their money (my idea of angels having now intirely vanifhed). When fuddenly, before I was aware, a tall, mafculine, Alæputa clafps me in her arms, mounts into the air, and flies with me about fifty paces; then fet me down, and run away laughing like to kill herfelf;

as did all that faw it. I own my furprife and fright was very confiderable, however when I recovered myfelf, the ridiculoufnefs of the thing moved my rifible faculties alfo. When my friend joined me, he defired I would feel my pockets, to fee if I had loft nothing, which upon examination was luckily found to be the cafe.

We fupped at Morogow's, where they laughed very heartily at my adventure. Before we feparated, a party was made to go next evening to one of the theatres, to fee a famous actor called Garrimond in one of Avonfwan's plays, which were conftantly brought here and tranflated. Bonaris undertook to fecure us places (which required confiderable intereft when

when that actor appeared); and we appointed to meet at a houfe of entertainment near the theatre.

We were engaged to dine the next day with the Queen's Ambaſſador at that court, who was alſo obliged to conform to the Luxo-voluptan manner of living. He ſeemed to be a man of ſuperior worth and abilities, and was much eſteemed. At table he was very affable and agreeable, and hearing of my adventure, was a good deal diverted. This turned the converſation upon ſo very extraordinary a particularity with reſpect to chaſtity; and many ſtories were told of jealous huſbands, and the means afforded by theſe wings of eſcaping detection. It afterwards fell on their manners in general. Their exceffive gaming, by which in a few years eftates of twenty thoufand gorgerines (equal to fo many of our guineas) yearly, were often reduced to little or nothing. The vaft fums of money thrown away in electing delegates to the lower houfe of Cortefinas or Parliament, with the great corruption both of the Electors and Elected. The great profufion of the public money, in place of the exact œconomy which a ftate fo much in debt required; like a fpendthrift heir, who, the more defperate his circumftances become, grows only the more extravagant. Their exceffive liberty degenerated into licentioufnefs. Their parties and factions are carried to fuch exceffive heights, and many other things

things too tedious to repeat; which in the opinion of the company, were ſtrong ſymptoms, that if ſome convulſion did not happen to reſtore to the Luxo-voluptans their former virtue, that they muſt ſoon deſtroy themſelves in anarchy and confuſion, or give up their liberties (at leaſt a part of them) to the crown, as the only remedy remaining to prevent their total deſtruction.

Three or four days after was appointed by the Ambaſſador, to introduce us at court; and he ſpoke very highly of Gorgeris the Monarch of this vaſt Empire, as he did alſo of her Majeſty, his royal conſort.

From the Ambaſſador's, we went to the appointed place for meeting; which had a public room, for the drinking of beverages, like our coffee, orgeat,

orgeat, &c. &c.; and it being too early to go to the Theatre, we amufed ourfelves with looking over the printed papers of news, which were in prodigious numbers; I counted thirty publifhed that day, and fuppofe thofe were not the whole. Moraveres addreffing himfelf to Bonaris, faid, he wondered what they could find worth reading to infert every day in thefe numerous fheets; and what effect they had upon their politics. The other replied, that they eafily found means to fill them with one thing or another; politics, fcandal, domeftic and foreign occurrences are inexhauftible topics; and if they are at a lofs, it is eafy making a lie; the contradicting of which next day will make another paragraph. As to the effect

they

they have upon our politics, continued he, it is hard to fay whether the liberty of the prefs does more good or harm. For on the one hand, if it deters Minifters from taking meafures which may infringe the liberties of the people; on the other, as the plaineft propofitions may be wrefted by an artful writer, to give a very unfair view of it, the people are very often mifled by them.

We now took our places in the Theatre; and until the play began, I was very well entertained with examining the houfe. It was of an immenfe fize (at leaft in comparifon with that at Ludorow), and having been lately fitted up by a celebrated Architect, was both elegant and magnificent. I was alfo not a little diverted with the pretty flutterings of
the

the Alæ-putas, who occupied principally some of the upper lodges, and frequently took wing from one side of the house to the other, when they saw a spark they wanted to draw into their snares.

When the curtain was drawn up, and Garrimond entered on the stage, there was a clapping of hands which continued for a minute or two; at last all was attention through the play, except when some sentiment or fine piece of action forced their applause. I had seen that very piece performed at Ludorow, under the direction of the author; and must do Garrimond the justice to own, that he seemed to understand his part perfectly; and though under the disadvantage of a translation, gave a greater force to the

character

character he played, than the actor who performed it at Ludorow. But at the Bonhommican theatre every part was equally well acted, which was far from being the cafe here; fo that (except one or two women) Garrimond appeared like a giant amongft dwarfs. If this actor has great merit, he has been alfo very fortunate to appear in a country where amufements are fo much the fafhion, and fo highly valued. By what I was informed, he has made ten times more money by acting Avonfwan's plays, than ever the author did by writing them; and to fuch a degree of frenzy has their admiration of him arofe, that had he a rival of equal merit, I make no doubt but the fcene of the famous pantomimes

of

of degenerated Rome would be renewed, and the nobility would take party, wear their liveries, and follow their triumphal cars.

We made up proper clothes to make our appearance in at court, and were introduced one after another to their Majesties, who received us very graciously, and we had the honour of kissing their hands. When it came to my turn to be presented to the King, his Excellency the Ambassador said, I was a native of a country on the other side the globe, who by a fatal accident had been left by the ship I came in; which had been sent out with another by our King to make discoveries in the southern hemisphere, and in a particular manner whether or not there was a great continent

continent on that fide of the globe. That I had made my way to Bonhommica through many dangers and adventures, where his Queen had been pleafed to take me into her fervice.

His Luxo-voluptan Majefty heard him with great attention, and afterwards talked to me above a quarter of an hour; afking very pertinent queftions concerning my country and its fovereign. His Majefty faid, he highly honoured the King of Great Britain for his liberality of fentiment, in fitting out fhips for the difcovery of unknown countries. That if ever I got home, I might affure his Majefty, if any fhips belonging to his fubjects fhould vifit the Luxo-voluptan ports, they might depend on the

ufage

uſage which the nations moſt favoured, and in greateſt friendſhip with his ſubjects, received.

It was ſoon buzzed about in the apartments, that I was of a nation on the other ſide of the world, when immediately a great curioſity was raiſed concerning me. I heard them ſay to one another, what is he like? Is he a rational creature? Let us go ſee him. When they found I was no monſter, and could ſpeak their language tolerably, I had ſoon a great circle round me of Nomras and Nomrinas, Comras and Comrinas (Gentlemen and Ladies), and even ſome Nomrihas and Nomrihinas (Dukes and Dutcheſſes), who aſked me a thouſand impertinent queſtions. I anſwered them as well as I could, and

and was glad when it was over; but this produced me many invitations to dinners and suppers, from the principal nobility; some of which I accepted, that an opportunity of learning something of their manners and customs might not be lost.

The first Luxo-voluptan I dined with, was a Nomra in a great post in administration. I need not say every thing was in the greatest grandeur and elegance. Some of the Nomrinas and Comrinas at table, seemed by their shoulders to be of the order of Gallanteras; but they were not the less censorious for that reason, perhaps on the contrary the more so, to hide their own blemishes. Several anecdotes from the scandalous chronicle were mentioned by them,

them, and one in particular which had happened two evenings before. A certain Nomrihina, whofe Nomriha was fo exceffively jealous, that he had clipped her wings, and confined her to his houfe. This made her meeting with her noble Corrumpero extremely difficult, But what, faid the Gallantera, cannot all-powerful love atchieve? her wings growing very faft, fhe fometimes converfed with him on the top of her own houfe, but more generally he was let in at a garret window by her maid, the confidante. But that evening the Nomriha her hufband got intelligence of their being together in the maid's chamber, and was fo near furprifing them, that the Corrumpero was obliged to fly out at the window in his fhirt, and has got fuch a cold that he keeps his bed;

bed, which has thrown the poor Nomrihina into immoderate affliction. Commend me, said another Gallantera, to the Faramondian manners, where though every husband has cause, none are jealous; it is not the fashion. And a most excellent fashion it is, rejoined a third; why should people, when they are tired of one another, pique themselves on a ridiculous constancy? No, continued she, give and take liberties on both sides, say I; it is the pleasure of life, and saves a great deal of uneasiness and ill humour, about a very trifling affair. I took the liberty of observing to that lady, that it must be a difficult thing in that country for people to know their fathers. Is it not so every where? replied she smartly; but of what confequence is that? they know their mothers, and that is fufficient. Pray Madam, rejoined I, do the Burghers in that country alfo follow the fafhion ? The Burghers, exclaimed fhe! No, if it defcended to them it would be enough to make people of quality almoft leave it off. The converfation afterwards changed to politics, and they talked much of the monftrous ingratitude of the Armoferians, a large colony of theirs at a thoufand leagues diftance, who had revolted. A Nomra faid, that after having nurfed them up to maturity at fo great an expence, and entered into a war folely on their account, by which the nation had incurred an additional debt of above fixty millions ; how unreafonable it was to expect, that the mother country

fhould

should continue to bear all the burden, when they were become so able to take a share of it. Besides, continued he, it would absolutely have been the ruin of the kingdom, by depopulating it; for who, but people of large property, would continue to live in this country, where every thing is taxed so high, when by going to Armoseria, they could enjoy a finer climate, and live at a quarter the expence, without reckoning the great advantages of making a fortune in a country not the twentieth part peopled? The great emigrations which took place since the end of last war, plainly evince this. Another Nomra rejoined, that if a certain tax which was laid on, had not been repealed by a former

admi-

adminiſtration, (the members of which were now violent in oppoſition), it would have executed itſelf, and we ſhould have had no rebellion. But the Armoſerians by that weakneſs were ſpirited up to oppoſe every tax that ſhould be laid on them ; thinking that non-importation would make ſuch a clamour among the Merchants, as to frighten the Miniſtry. A Comra of the lower houſe of Corteſinas was of opinion that the error lay deeper, even in the very original Charters of the Colonies, which by giving them a conſtitution ſimilar to that of the mother country, made them imagine they did not depend on the Corteſinas, but only on the King. The poſterity of a ſet of determined rupublicans, ſaid he, ſhould have been
held

held in with a tighter rein; efpecially when they were yearly reinforced with fuch a virtuous fet of recruits from every jail in the kingdom: fome of whofe defcendants, for any thing we know, may be now leading-men in the congrefs. Opinions on this affair were perfectly unanimous in this company.

The next I dined with was alfo a Nomra, but who had been turned out of a great office. Here the fentiments were diametrically oppofite to the former company, concerning the Armoferians; and they all agreed that they were the moft oppreffed and ill-ufed people under the fun. What! the Cortefinas to tax a people contrary to their inclinations, who are not reprefented! was ever any thing heard of so unconstitutional? What signifies your having nursed, and defended them, at the expence of sixty millions of gorgerines, till they are grown powerful enough to go to war with you; if you will now take their money from them without their consent? Surely the mother country gets enough by her exclusive trade with them, said they (which is now the only one she can depend on), without thinking of taxing her own children.

An evening or two after, I was at the house of one of our worthy Merchants, with a set of Bonhommicans and Bonaris. In the course of the conversation, I happened to mention the very different sentiments I had heard concerning the Armoserian rebellion;

rebellion; when the whole company joined with me in defiring Bonaris to explain that matter to us. It needs no other, replied he, than that the one is out of place, and the other is in. What, exclaimed a Bonhommican! does that alter the nature of the thing? Entirely, faid the other; for if they were to change fituations (which may poffibly foon be the cafe), they would immediately change their opinions and manner of fpeaking, both in public and private. Good God! cried another; can men have the impudence to act in fuch a barefaced manner? Very eafily, returned Bonaris, we fee it every day; they find out fubterfuges and equivocations; and at the worft, if one has been in an error, is he always to perfift in it? But, faid a third, are not they defpifed by every body?——Only by the party they have quitted,—— the other receives them with open arms. If a man indeed pretends to ftand neuter, continued Bonaris, upon motives of confcience, he is fhunned and defpifed by both. What is very extraordinary, there are many honeft men among them (of both parties), in the common intercourfes of life; but they get fo heated by their difputes, that one would think they actually forgot the difference betwixt right and wrong. In this affair of the Armoferians, continued he, I own the oppofition carried things a little too far; for by their fpeeches in the Cortefinas, printed pamphlets, and writings in the news-papers (there being fome great names amongft them), the rebels were fpirited up,

by

by thinking they had their approbation, and expecting a diversion made at home in their favour. By this means they have probably been led by degrees to carry things farther than they at first intended, and at last to the greatest extremities, which will ruin millions of these people, and cost this country much blood and immense treasure. Too far, cried they with one voice! why were not they punished?——They generally took care to keep clear of the laws against high treason, which are very favourable in this country; and where some words might be construed as such, the government thought proper to overlook them, for fear of raising disturbances. Thought I to myself, a little of Queen Tudorina's government

ment would do this Nation no harm, no more than Old England.

I dined another day with a Nomra who did not feem much involved in politics, and happening to ftay after every other perfon was gone, he offered to carry me with him to his club. I afked him, what kind of meeting it was? O! fays he, you fhall go and fee a little of our manners, though we are a felect body, and none can be admitted without being ballotted for; yet fuch a ftranger as you are, there can be no objection to! You muft know, fays he, that clubs are kept among the men of all degrees in this Metropolis, it is the general cuftom; but there are about a fcore called fo by way of eminence,

eminence, which are only compofed of the Nomras and Comras of diftinction. And how do you employ yourfelves there, rejoined I? We eat and drink in the moft elegant manner at a fmall expence, returned he, it not cofting us above two gorgerines a head for dinner or fupper; then we fport our money pretty freely at different games. We are very numerous, continued he, and we are confequently fure of always finding company whenever we have an inclination to go. But, rejoined I, do not fome of you get devilifh tumbles fometimes? O yes, anfwered he, we are all in debt, but the Nation owes two hundred millions, fo it is the fafhion you fee. Give me leave to afk you only one queftion more, faid I: How do your wives difpofe of
themfelves

themselves while you are at your clubs? O, the best way they can, replied he, we do not trouble ourselves about that. There has indeed been an attempt made to establish one where both sexes are admitted, but it does not take, it is unnatural.

We found between forty and fifty people in a large handsome room, well illuminated, amusing themselves at different games of cards and dice. They were all men of fortune and fashion, of the upper or lower house of Cortesinas, and many of them in high offices; but all had the same passion for sporting their money; that is to say, were not contented with what they had, and wishing to increase it at the expence of another. Those who were not much engaged,

sat

sat down to a very elegant supper at midnight. After that, things went on with more spirit, the company gradually increasing. I shall not pretend to describe this scene, great sums were won and lost, and the floor was entirely covered with cards; but in the height of it, a small accident discomposed them a little for a short time.

Whilst two Nomras were playing at a game, something resembling Picquet, one of them was suddenly attacked with an apoplectic fit; he was immediately removed into another room by the waiters, and proper medical assistance sent for. But before he went, the Nomra who had played with him desired the company to take notice (in case of his antagonist's nift's recovery), that he had the game in his hand. Towards morning they gradually dropped off, and returned home, jaded with want of reft; the lofers in all the horrors of defpair and vexation, and the winners enjoying not half the fatisfaction which might be imagined. The place of a principal waiter at one of thefe clubs, is more lucrative than a good poft under government; for befides the profufe gratuities they receive for their attendance, they are bankers to the winners, and ufurious lenders to the lofers, becoming fo opulent, that they are fometimes elected into the lower houfe of Cortefinas; where they are careffed by, and fit on the fame bench with thofe, behind whofe chairs they formerly ftood. When I confidered the manner of life thefe

Luxo-voluptans conftantly led, I was not furprifed that the women's wings grew, and flourifhed exceedingly.

The women not being lefs curious than the men to learn the manners, cuftoms, and virtues of the Englifh, I was alfo much careffed by them, and carried to fome affemblies where none but felect company were admitted. There I could fee that play was equally their paffion as that of the other fex, though it did not run near fo high; a gorgerine a fifh, at a game refembling our quadrille, and high ftakes at another, like our loo, fufficiently agitated at times their beautiful features. All back feathers were carefully concealed at thefe meetings, as well as at routes, which the women frequently gave at their own

own houses. In these last, it seemed to be their great ambition, to make them as disagreeable to themselves and the company as they possibly could, by crouding their apartments as full as they could hold.

But though back feathers were concealed, some of the head wings were enormous. I asked a Comrina, whom I had the honour to be known to (at one of the latter places); how she proposed spending her evening. She replied, that after dining at the Nomra such a one's, they had gone to the play, from the play here; from hence to two more routes, from thence to rondelleva, from rondelleva to fairy-hall where they sup, and from thence home. At what time may the last happen? resumed I,—it was

was impossible to say exactly; perhaps between five and six, returned she.

Having already mentioned my being fond of music, and even a performer, it will be expected that the concerts and operas were not wholly neglected by me. The best voices and performers on instruments there, as well as in London, are foreigners. The music is very much in the Italian taste, and they have many great composers; but whether they or the Italians ought to be preferred, I shall not take upon me to determine.

The entertainment however which surprised and diverted us most, was a masked ball given at the Theopan, a large rotunda lately built in a beautiful stile of architecture. We were told there would not be another while

while we stayed at Miro-volante, and as none of the other commanders nor myself had ever seen one, we made a party of which Bonaris was one, and went to it in Ma gelores, a dress resembling what they call Dominos in the shops of Taviftock-Street. As this ball was open to every one for their money, all the different species of human flyers were in great plenty, and made at least four-fifths of the whole company; there the Galanteras and Corrumperos (as their faces were concealed) gave themselves no trouble to hide their wings, however eafily it might have been done from their fmallnefs. It was very ridiculous to obferve the different growths of them, upon the fhoulders of tall men and women. Some were only of a fize for Genii or Cupids,

Cupids, and they increased gradually to that of Angels or Devils. The greatest number were of the last, and it was only those which could support the body in a flight of any extent. They were of all colours, and many of them kept in excellent order; but I was sorry to see a great many hoary ones, which looked as if they would preserve them to their last breath. It was not easy to discern the difference of sexes, but by what we could judge, the females were greatly the majority. They were all dressed in imitation of different birds, with proper masks resembling their heads, and very well imitated.

Think how laughable a scene it must have been, to see such a number of tame birds (though often of the refemblance of wild ones) flying, hopping, chattering and fqueaking about the room. Some of the Alæ-putas would fly up to the top of the dome, and fkim round it, expofing a little too much their lower parts; but I muft do them the juftice to fay, that they all wore drawers. A few of the Gallanteras and their imitators brought their carrs and equipage with them in their chairs, in which they alfo flew about in a more decent manner, to the great entertainment of the company. To defcribe the outrages done to nature, in that ftrange group of feathered rationals, would be endlefs. Hawks gallanting hen pheafants, vultures turkey hens, and eagles pea-hens. Crows arm in arm with white pigeons, fcreech owls with nightingales, and ravens with

with Chinese pheasants. But what diverted us more particularly after supper and the wine had gone freely about, was, to see a mild turtle-dove cuffing a goss hawk very smartly round the room. They at last became a little too riotous, and we left them before four o'clock.

Our evening's diversion had like to have had melancholy consequences. The worthy Moraveres our Quadorow, was taken ill of a fever two days after; whether occasioned by catching cold, the hurry and croud of the place, or from what other cause, it was impossible to say. We were alarmed for him, and proposed calling in a physician, which he for some time opposed, hoping it would go off; but finding it did not, he at last consented.

confented. The queftion now was, which one to fend for. Morrogow and Nicophange propofed Nicopheris, the one they employed for ordinary in their families, and had reafon to be fatisfied with. The other commanders and myfelf were for one of greater note and more extenfive practice. The matter was referred to Bonaris, our oracle in moft things, who faid, that in the practice of phyfic in Miro-volante, there was a diftinction to be made, between the art and the fcience. That the art confifted in being well with as many apothecaries as poffible, by prefcribing great quantities of fuperfluous medicines for their benefit; in fetting themfelves off to the beft advantage, efpecially with the women; in recounting remarkable cures performed by by themselves, no matter though not entirely confiftent with truth; in fhewing a very particular concern for, and attention to their patients diforder. In vifiting at uncommon hours, continued Bonaris, from their great anxiety and care, and giving very minute directions to nurfes, as if the leaft particular was of confequence, chufing always to have them of their own recommendation, as it was their intereft to fpeak well of them. I am very fenfible (ftill continued he), that fome of the phyficians in high reputation have acquired it meerly by their merit; but there are alfo a great number who have pufhed themfelves by arts like the above mentioned; fuch arts are not practifed by Nicopheris, he is above them; but he is a very learned and knowing phyſician, and in my opinion Moraveres cannot be in better hands. He was accordingly ſent for, and we had no reaſon to repent of it. In a few days our friend by his care was out of danger; and ſoon recovered entirely, to the great ſatisfaction of us all.

While Moraveres was in danger, we ſeldom ſtirred abroad; and Bonaris frequently calling in upon us, I had a great deal of converſation with him upon the kingdom of Luxovolupto, and their neighbours on that continent. The ſouthern continent, he ſaid, conſiſted of ſeveral powerful kingdoms, two of whom, Caſtillaria and Faramondia; had, at different periods, aimed at univerſal Monarchy; but both had failed, from the other

other nations uniting againſt them. In which alliances, the Luxo-voluptans had acted a very diſtinguiſhed part, eſpecially in the laſt againſt Faramondia; who being their neareſt neighbour, had of conſequence always been their natural enemy. In this vigorous exertion (he continued), they fell into the pernicious cuſtom of borrowing money on the national faith; which, by degrees, had involved them in an enormous debt, with little probability of its ever being paid off. The other great kingdoms, he ſaid, had all loſt their liberty; the Luxo-voluptans alone having preſerved theirs (after many ſtruggles with their Monarchs), by their virtue, and love of freedom. That after the laſt great exertion in behalf of it, the

boundary

boundary was fixed between the prerogative of the crown, and the rights of the people; since which time, no nation was ever happier, or at least had more just cause to be so. But trade and manufactures having brought immence wealth into the country, luxury followed fast on their steps; whose strides have been much lengthened by the conquest of a rich and manufacturing country at eight thousand leagues distance, by a company of Merchants. The servants of that company (still continued he), have been guilty of such rapacity on the natives, as shocks humanity to think of; and come home with immense fortunes, which, as they got them so easily, they spend wantonly.

Our

Our immense colonies are grown also extremely rich and powerful. A war which was entered into entirely on their account, terminated, as was generally thought, gloriously; by having a large country which lay behind them ceded to us. But now they were freed from their only enemy, they soon shewed their refractory spirit, and at length broke out into an open rebellion; are now carrying on war against their mother-country; and how that will terminate, there is yet no making any judgment. Wealth is become the only object which all men aim at to support that luxury, and all crimes of course are perpetrated to attain it. That spirit of liberty which still remains, said Bonaris, has degenerated into licentiousness; especially in that quarter of Miro-volante called the City; where valuing themselves on their riches, they make a point of opposing the court on all occasions; and become the dupes of every adventurer, who puts on the mask of Patriotism to deceive them.

It is, continued he, happy for us, that Faramondia is very near in as much debt, and as luxurious as ourselves, without having so good credit to borrow; otherwise we should not be long at peace with them. The above was the substance of what I learned from him in several conversations, and in the last, he gave a general character of that people in few words, but which, he said, must be understood with great allowances.

That

That the Nomras and Comras run out their fortunes without preserving their dignity. That the Nomrinas and Comrinas had almost given up all pretensions to chastity. That Religion and Morality had lost their influence on all ranks of people. And that a universal profligacy pervaded the whole.

Moraveres was now perfectly recovered from his illness; when a great mob paraded through the city, ordering every body to put out lights in their windows, in honour of the election of Wilkiferis, a great favourite of theirs, to an office of the greatest trust and profit in the city. I am extremely glad of it, cried out Bonaris. Who is he, said Moraveres? A very clever profligate, replied the
other,

other, who has known how to dupe thefe wifeacres for fome years paſt, and they have now put it in his power to do it effectually. While we were talking, an inferior Bonhommican officer came haſtily into the room, and acquainted the Quadarow, that the mob had fallen upon, and were abuſing many of their feamen, who happened to be on ſhore. We all went out immediately, and I heard fome of the mob faying one to another, " Damn thefe foreigners, what bufinefs have they here"? they pretend to be virtuous ; damn their virtue, will it bring them any thing? will it make the pot boil?

The Quadarow was obliged to apply to the chief magiſtrate, who got together a number of conſtables, and

and rescued them. They were all ordered on board immediately, and few for the future were suffered to come into the city.

CHAP.

CHAP. VIII.

Law. A Criminal Trial. Some account of the Country. Miro-volante. Army. Fleet. Manufactures. Court. Dress. Language. Clergy. Learning. Hospitals. Summer Amusements. Summer Theatre. Rondelleva. Fairy Hall. Horse Race.

THE Commanders, Bonaris, and myself, walked one day to the immense Hall, where the courts of justice are held. The courts were then sitting, and the crouds in all of them very great. We conversed with several people concerning the judges, who all agreed in praising their impartiality and justice; and many of them for their great abilities; especially

cially one of the chiefs, who was said to be a prodigy of knowledge and eloquence. Bonaris met an able counsellor of his acquaintance, whom he engaged to dine with us after the courts were up, at a house of entertainment hard by. He came according to his promise, and proved a frank agreeable companion. After dinner, when we were drinking a moderate glass, Mocophage (commander of one of the frigates), first making an apology for the liberty he was going to take, asked the counsellor in what compass the Luxovoluptan laws might be contained. In about a hundred volumes in folio, replied he: Good God! cried the other, how is it possible ever to learn them all? They never are, returned the counsellor; he who knows a third part

part of them is very deep. Give me leave to trouble you with another queſtion, ſaid the commander. How long are your law ſuits permitted to laſt? Sometimes ſeven years, and at others twenty or thirty, anſwered the lawyer.——And what is the reaſon of ſuch delays?——The glorious obſcurity of the law, replied he laughing. ——In my opinion you had better be without laws altogether:——Yes, ſaid he; the nation had, but not the lawyers. This dialogue diverted us.—— When Mocophage, in a ſerious but polite manner, ſaid, there muſt be great faults ſomewhere; and in his opinion, if the lawyers honeſtly told their clients that they had not right on their ſide, they certainly would not be mad enough to perſiſt in their ſuit, at a great expence, and often to

their

their utter ruin. In anfwer to which, the counfellor faid, it was not always an eafy matter to determine in what light things would appear to a judge, and ftill more fo to a jury; befides they were feldom confulted on the merits, and very often did not read their briefs till they came into court. ——And what is the reafon of that? ——Want of time, returned he.—— Your attornies muft then be very faulty.——That is the general opinion, but we cannot help that. Why are not they punifhed, faid the Bonhommican?——Becaufe they take care not to expofe themfelves to it. But to be ferious, continued the counfellor, our laws are certainly become a great nuifance, and want reformation; but it is fo arduous an undertaking, that it is not probable any

King or Miniſtry will venture on it, unleſs obliged by ſome fatal neceſſity. The Bonhommican laws were mentioned to ſhew the poſſibility of it; to which the counſellor anſwered,—That they were a virtuous people, who could do better without laws in any form whatſoever, than the Luxo-voluptans could with laws made on purpoſe for them by the deity, and ſent to them from the divine abodes. He added, that if their government ſhould have the misfortune to become deſpotic, a reformation might be eaſier brought about ; but that the remedy would be worſe than the diſeaſe.

The converſation then turned on debtors, and it was generally allowed, that though in juſtice debts ought to be be paid, if there was wherewithall; yet where there was not, imprisonment was depriving the creditors of any chance in future, and when they had not a proper maintenance, they had better be put to death at once. The counfellor acknowledged that the allowance in their prifons was but a meer trifle, and not always paid. What number of debtors, faid Moraveres, may be in the prifons of Mirovolante? He replied, Perhaps ten or twelve thoufand, but that he could not fay how many with any exactnefs. Good God! exclaimed the other, how fhocking to humanity that is! if the creditors were obliged to maintain them in a decent manner, they would not be fo ready to confine their perfons. In Ludorow, where that is done, there is not perhaps above one for each

each of your thoufands, but the different fizes of the cities and manners of the people muft alfo be taken into the account. The lawyer concluded the fubject with faying, that there was one advantage in making arrefts for debt eafily obtainable; that it facilitated credit. From debtors, it was a natural enough tranfition to criminals, and many queftions were afked of our communicative lawyer, concerning criminal laws and punifhments; which after he had anfwered in the moft explicit manner, he told us there was to be a very curious trial in two days, at the Criminal Court of a woman called Rudera, for forgery. That the affair had made a great noife for fome months, two of her accomplices being at that time under fentence of death. He was intreated

to

to give us a hiftory of the affair, which he did in the following manner.

" This Rudera has a hufband alive, whom fhe has ruined by her extravagance, has left for fome years, and lived with feveral other men· The laft of whom, and a friend of his, fhe was concerned with, in forging bonds for confiderable fums of money. That friend was detected in endeavouring to raife money on one of them, and, to excufe himfelf, faid, he got it from her; fhe being fent for, acknowledged herfelf guilty; but they were not then taken up. Afterwards when they were, fhe had art enough to get herfelf admitted as evidence for the king. But the principal profecutor, upon examining into the affair, finding that fhe was the chief contriver and perpetrator of the forgeries, and that he had proof enough againſt the others without her evidence, profecuted her alſo. Her plea was, that having been admitted king's evidence, fhe was not liable to be tried. It was argued by counſel before the principal court, and given againſt her; becauſe on her examination when admitted evidence for the King, fhe had not made a full difcovery.

" When fhe came to her trial ſome months ago, fhe made uſe of the ſame plea, and one of her judges had a ſcruple in his mind upon the legality of it. That occaſioned the trial's being put off, and the point of law's being referred to the twelve judges, who have again given it againſt

against her; and though nobody doubts of her guilt, yet, as she had been admitted an evidence, a kind of compaſſion has aroſe in the minds of men, as is common in this country, on the leaſt appearance of hardſhip or oppreſſion. And though in ſome countries, torture is made uſe of to make criminals confeſs their crimes, the laws are ſo favourable in this, that an extrajudicial confeſſion does not operate againſt them.

As we declared our reſolution of ſeeing this famous trial, he told us how we were to manage to get admittance, and adviſed us to be there early. We then parted, after having thanked bim for his agreeable company, and very judicious communications.

We did not fail being in court in proper time, and got places where we could both fee and hear perfectly well. Rudera entered the auguft tribunal with great modefty, yet with a fort of dignity. She was dreffed in an elegant fimplicity, very proper for her fituation. Her figure was genteel, but her face not remarkably handfome. The trial was long and folemn; during the whole of which, fhe behaved with fo much propriety, compofure, and feeming innocence, that all eyes were upon her, all wifhes for her acquittal. I own honeftly my being carried away with the torrent, but thought I perceived by the looks of my friends, that they were not equally prejudiced in her favour. She did not truft entirely to her counfel in crofs-examining the

witneffes,

witnesses, but was every now and then handing little billets to them with her inftructions. When it came to her defence, fhe made a fhort, but very proper fpeech, with much grace and modefty. The judges gave an impartial charge to the jury, explaining to them the laws in thefe cafes; and according as the proofs appeared to them, directing what their verdict fhould be. The jury were inclofed, and every one waited with anxiety and impatience for the event. But when fhe was pronounced Not guilty, there were the loudeft, and moft indecent fhouts of applaufe, that perhaps ever were heard in a court of juftice.

We got out as foon as the croud would permit us, and in our way home,

home, I imagined my friends were little fatisfied with what they had been witneffes to. I was not miftaken; for when the Merchants afked their opinions of what had paffed, they declared they had never feen fo utter a depravation, and even triumph over the moral fenfe as in the prifoner; nor fuch a total want of it, joined to a falfe pity and mifplaced generofity, as in the fpectators. Not, faid they, that we had any wifhes for her condemnation, let the laws take their courfe; but for fo crouded a court to feem unanimoufly folicitous for the acquittal of a perfon, of whofe guilt they had not the leaft doubt; feemed to them fo great an encouragement to commit crimes, that they were not furprifed to find them fo common in Miro-volante.

This

This trial was at what they call Juasforreris or gaol-delivery, which is held in this capital every six weeks. We were told when it was over, that at this seffions one hundred prisoners were tried; thirty of whom were condemned to suffer death, fifty to row in the gallies, and the rest were either whipped, branded, or acquitted. Such executions are not uncommon in this capital, they string up men with as little ceremony as a fish-woman does pilchards; neither the sufferers nor spectators seeming to give themselves much concern about it.

The crimes which were most general, were highway robberies, housebreakings, forgeries, thefts and frauds. Few murders or rapes were found in their seffions paper.

Having

Having made feveral excurfions to different parts of this country, feen the greateft part of the metropolis, and obtained information concerning their military and naval eftablifhments, manufactures, &c. &c. I fhall now give a fhort account of them.

The foil in general is good, highly cultivated, and the country almoft every where inclofed; there are fome large diftricts however, that are mountainous and barren, efpecially the remote parts to the fouthward. The inhabitants of that country are poor when compared with the others; but the keen air of their mountains fharpens their wits, and many of them migrate northward to better their fortunes in a warmer foil, in which they fometimes

times succeed; for the northern inhabitants are a good-natured people, and receive with open arms those who readily fall in with their manners. But sometimes they find these friends a little too far south for them.

Navigable canals are numerous, and extremely beneficial to trade; the excellent roads also, which have been made within half a century at an immense expence (by a heavy tax laid on carriages and horses which pass over them), concur to the same good end; as well as to the ease and conveniency of travellers. They actually very much approximate places to one another, and a journey which could not formerly be made under a fortnight, with great trouble and fatigue (the persons making their

wills

wills before they set out), is now performed with ease and pleasure in two or three days. The only inconvenience to be feared from this luxurious way of travelling (for the Inns are equally good with the roads) is, that as all ranks of people are now conveyed on carriages of one sort or other, inside or outside; their bodies will be so enervated, that in time they may become incapable of supporting the hardships and fatigues of war. For I have heard that the fox-hunters, who used to be the hardiest riders in the kingdom, go now to the field in post chaises (if their sport lies at any distance from home), mount their horses there, and return in the same vehicle, or a hired one, if the chase carries them to a great distance from it.

†   Miro-

· Miro-volante confifts of two Cities, and for its fize might very well make ten very confiderable ones. It is twenty-four miles in circuit, and contains above a million of inhabitants. There are above twenty large fquares, but fuch of them as have ftatues, are far from being embellifhed by them. Three ftone bridges, two of which are modern, and noble pieces of architecture; the third antient (though lately vamped up at nearly as much expence as would have rebuilt it), a ftructure of an ignorant age, the piers being built on piles which rife up above low water mark. The Arches are fmall, irregular, and barbarous; and the ftream ftill more ftreightened by ftarlings filled with large ftones placed round the bottoms of the peers, to prevent their being under-

undermined; fo that many lives are loft yearly, in paffing under it from the great fall. It is, in brief, offenfive to the eye, hurtful to Navigation, and deftructive of the human race. The Temples are numerous and magnificent, one of which, for greatnefs and beauty, might vie with any in the world. This city is of late well paved at the expence of two millions of gorgerines, and is lighted by 100,000 globular lamps. But what furprifes one moft with refpect to this Capital is, that they are ftill extending it on all fides; go where you will on the out-fkirts, there is nothing to be feen but new buildings; without any ones being able to conceive where any additional inhabitants are to come from. But the builders (from experience) depend on the reftlefs ficklenefs of the Luxovoluptans;

vóluptans; well knowing that any new fafhioned manner of fitting them up; fuch as a little Painting, or fome plafter figures on the ceiling or walls of the rooms (though the houfes in general are not fo convenient), will certainly draw the inhabitants to them. So that it is probable, in a few years, more than one-third of the houfes will be left uninhabited. The Palace, which ftruck me moft from the harbour at our firft arrival, on account of its grandeur and magnificence, was originally begun for a royal one, and after being much enlarged, was converted into an Hofpital for fuperannuated feamen. There is another very fine one, but much inferior to the abovementioned, in poffeffion of the invalids of the land fervice. I have afked

feveral

several of the old men at both Palaces, if they were not very happy to pass the remainder of their days in such superb structures. Their answer constantly was, that they would willingly give up all the grandeur of their habitations, for half a penuris a day additional allowance, to buy them a weed resembling our tobacco.

Several other Hospitals for variety of purposes, are likewise unnecessarily ornamented. The Charity of the Luxo-voluptans is very ostentatious. But one of the oldest and meanest public buildings in this great Metropolis is the Royal Palace, which is indeed utterly unworthy of its great inhabitant, and of the Empire. But the Cortesinas will not let themselves conceive,

ceive, that their Monarch can be capable of the same weakness with his subjects, of liking a new house better than an old one.

This kingdom has now a very numerous body of troops in Armoseria, but in time of peace it is customary for them to keep up a standing army of 20,000 infantry and 8,000 cavalry; besides 6,000 guards, who are always quartered in the capital. Their troops make a good appearance, and are said always to fight well; though they are generally the most debauched, profligate fellows in the kingdom.

They have at present a very formidable fleet in commission, consisting of about thirty ships of the line of battle, and above one hundred frigates. They are by far the moſt potent maritime power in that part of the globe; but, on infpecting their ſhips, I did not find them much fuperior to the Bonhommicans, either in ſhip-building, the art of navigation, or in the conſtruction of their fire-arms. It is on very great emergencies indeed, that they are ever obliged to make ufe of the odious meafure of preſſing feamen, to man their fleets. The operation of two very fimple laws, with a moderate bounty, generally anfwer that end. The firſt law is, that if any owners of Merchant ſhips give more wages to their feamen, than what is half an ecuris per month, under the King's pay (which is fomething higher than the

the British), the ship and cargo are forfeited, half to go to the informer. By this law, the freight of goods is also kept moderate in time of war, by preventing the rise of seamen's wages in the Merchant service. The second is, that every seaman has a right to demand his discharge at the end of two years; but if he happens to be abroad, and it would be a detriment to the service to part with him, he is intitled for the first six months, to half an ecuris per month additional; for the second six months an ecuris per month, for the third three half ecuris, and so on. Their sailors are reckoned brave, but unthinking like our English Tars.

Though the Luxo-voluptans have got very little the start of the Bonhommicans in naval arts, they certainly

tainly far excel them in many of their manufactures and mechanical ones. Their filks, velvets, and gold and filver ftuffs are beautiful, and fumptuous; and their houfehold furniture in a grand tafte and well executed. This gives the court of Mirovolante, a much gawdier appearance than that of Ludorow, but without half its dignity.

It is impoffible to give a defcription of the drefs worn by people of fafhion and their imitators, as it changes its appearance almoft as often, though not with the fame regularity, as the moon does hers: it being the chief ftudy of the Taylors, Mantua-makers, and Milleners, &c. in greateft reputation (as well as of the Beaux, Belles, and Alæ-putas), to

invent

invent new modes of it, befides what they copy from the Faramondians. This is faid to be greatly advantageous to trade, and for the fame fpecious reafon, the time for wearing mourning for deceafed relations is indecently fhortened; but they (and others of inferior rank) never fail to put it on for the death of any foreign Prince, whofe name perhaps they never before heard of, if it is to be wore only for a week.

I never heard that any of the richeft Nomrihas (though fome have 50,000 gorgerines of yearly rent) were above receiving the falaries of their offices; they have no notion of ferving either King or Country *gratis*, or perhaps are afraid of affronting them by a refufal.

As to the language of this nation, it is in a medium betwixt the foftnefs of the Auditantine, and roughnefs of the Bonhommican. It is fmooth enough to be fet to mufic, and yet both nervous and copious.

It has been already faid, that the Seraphite religion is profeffed here, as well as in Bonhommica; the only difference being, that a Hierarchy is eftablifhed in this kingdom, and confequently the priefts enjoy a confiderable fhare of power and wealth. Their Temples alfo are more magnificent, and more ornamented; but without any thing tending to idolatry.

Our worthy commanders conftantly went to one Temple or other, on the days appointed for public worfhip; and

and they ufed often with great concern, to lament the general neglect of religion in this country; very few attending on thefe occafions, and thofe who did, with great levity and unconcern.

But what was ftill more melancholy, the priefts themfelves did not fhew much fervour or piety, when exercifing their facred functions; but haftened them over as a tafk which muft be gone through.

This became the fubject of converfation one evening, when Moraveres addreffing himfelf to Bonaris, faid, he imagined their priefts thought more of obtaining good livings and dignities, than of ferving the Deity as they ought. He was forry to fay, Bonaris replied, that it was too true, but

but they were but men; and it was natural to wish, and endeavour to be in easy circumstances; nor did he see how it could be prevented.——By putting a check, returned the other, to the lust of riches and power, a the first setting out, as is done in Bonhommica. They would be then obliged to turn their ambition to the gaining of respect from their virtue and good life; since they could not have it from their wealth and dignity. ——But, rejoined Bonaris, would not that check the praise-worthy emulation of distinguishing themselves? and (as men enter into the priesthood for a livelihood, as they do into other professions) prevent those of spirit and genius from engaging in it.—— I do not think that men of spirit and genius make the best priests, said Moraveres,

Moraveres, but am rather of the contrary opinion. As to the checking of emulation, I grant that preferment is a fpur to the exertion of talents, which otherwife might never have been known. But on the other hand, when a man has once got at his eafe, he grows lazy, and his time is more agreeably employed in enjoying the goods of fortune, than in hard ftudy. In our country, continued he, the priefts are allowed a decent competency from the ftate; putting them much above contempt, but by no means in affluence. Therefore, though by writing they can do themfelves no fervice in the way of preferment, yet the Prefs may afford them fome affiftance to help their income; and increafe at the fame time their reputation. Moraveres being here filent,

a paufe

a paufe enfued for fome little time; when Bonaris refuming the difcourfe, faid to Moraveres, But perhaps you approve of our Devotionalifts, who, though profeffing themfelves of the eftablifhed religion, pretend to an extraordinary piety; who neglect their duty to themfelves, their families, and to fociety, to run about after religious exercifes; and are either puffed up with an impious affurance, of being in favour with the Deity, or depreffed with terrors of having offended him. Moraveres replied, That curiofity had led him to attend their meetings, and though he fincerely pitied them, he was far from approving the ftrange opinions they held, concerning the attributes of the Deity, of grace being all-fufficient without good works; and that
every

every one who did not think as they do, was in a ftate of reprobation, with other doctrines which were fubverfive of morality and true religion. That he believed their Teachers were either artful hypocrites, or filly enthufiafts; the former deferving punifhment, and the latter confinement in a mad-houfe. Bonaris declared, he intirely agreed with him in his opinion of them; but, faid he, let us return to our own Priefts, who I fhould be happy to defend, or at leaft offer fomething in extenuation of their conduct; and I am apt to believe, that it is not fo much the church government, that makes the priefts of one nation, more exemplary than that of another, as the manners of the people amongft whom they live; and the education they receive

in

in common with others, in their infancy. For, continued he, how can a Bonhommican make a bad prieſt, who does every thing conſcientiouſly? But, purſued he, we muſt mend our manners in general, to procure the particular reformation we have been talking of; and I am afraid there is little probability of that happening, without ſome humiliating reverſe of fortune. Education might do much, if children at the ſame time could be preſerved from the bad examples of all about them. But we go on in the old way, of teaching them nothing but two dead languages all the early part of their lives, taking little care of cultivating the moral ſenſe, and yet are ſurpriſed that our people are not as virtuous as yours.

The

The Bonhommicans all agreed, that if their favourite sense was not early rooted, and thoroughly fortified, all the care in the world afterwards, would have little effect; for all mankind had the seeds of it in their bosoms, though it was only in theirs, and in those of a few individuals of other nations, that its fruit grew up to maturity. Your universities, said they, may be better than ours with respect to the sciences, and what is called learning in general, but they will be able to do little in morality.

As to our Colleges, answered Bonaris, they have produced very great men, and there are still some of considerable learning amongst them, but at present none very remarkable.

The profefforfhips are too well endowed to expect any confiderable exertions from that quarter, and indeed fcarcely one of them gives a lecture: The education of youth is then intrufted to Tutors, who carry them through all the different branches of learning. Judge you, continued he, whether one man can be capable of doing it as it ought to be. In other refpects the difcipline is fo loofe, that a young fellow may there indulge himfelf in debauchery with great fecurity, if he is not guilty of any very open breach of decorum. And yet, faid Mocophage, learning in general, the fciences and arts, are at prefent in high reputation amongft you? They are fo, rejoined Bonaris, and very juftly; but not owing fo fo much to the Univerfities, as to fome other

other Societies, and the application of private men. The Royal Scientifical Club has promoted moſt of them in a very high degree, and ſtill keeps up to the ſpirit and vigour of its inſtitution. Other private ones, on ſimilar, or different plans, both in the capital and other principal cities of the Empire, have alſo done their part. And the royal ſchool of arts lately inſtituted, promiſes fair to raiſe Painting, Sculpture, and Architecture, to a very high degree of perfection.

You ſee, my friends, continued he, I endeavour to be as impartial as poſſible; the defects in our manners are too glaring, not to be eaſily ſeen by one who ſearches after truth.

Upon this I obſerved to him, That the many Hoſpitals which had been erected

erected in Miro-volante within half a century paſt, ſeemed to demonſtrate, that a laudable charity ſtill exiſted in the breaſts of his countrymen in general; and that (according to my religion) charity covered a multitude of ſins. He replied, That there had indeed been a number of new erected Hoſpitals; but the motives on which the erectors proceeded, made the merit of ſuch actions. That ſometimes it was difficult to penetrate into the receſſes of the human heart, and at others eaſy enough. One or two, which had been built and endowed by particular perſons, ſeemed plainly with an intention to raiſe a name; as mean and deſpicable a piece of vanity as any the human mind is ſubject to, and where they have valuable relations, far from praiſe-worthy.

worthy. As to thofe, continued he, which have been built and fupported by fubfcription, I know for a certainty, that the projectors of many of them had felfifh views; and it is not improbable, but the contributors acted more, from an eafinefs of temper, oftentation, the convenience of fending their fervants to them, or fome other motive, than from true benevolence of heart.

The converfation now turned to variety of fubjects; when, after fometime, Moraveres addreffing himfelf to Bonaris, faid, The Cortefinas is now broke up, and all your Nomras and Comras gone into the country; be fo obliging to let me know how both fexes pafs their time in it? Do they refide at their country-feats, and keep

hofpitality,

hospitality, as ours do at that season? Bonaris smiled and answered, Very, very few I assure you: they have got such a habit of dissipation and idleness, that they would grow low-spirited, if left in the country with only their friends about them. But there are, continued he, about twenty spaws in different parts of the kingdom, and as many sea-bathing places upon the coast, which are all full of company, not one in twenty of whom go for their healths; every one of these places has a ball-room or two, where they play cards from morning till night, and dance as often as they chuse. Besides those, there are horse races once every summer (and oftener in some) in almost every town in the kingdom; at which there are cock-fightings for the men, and balls

balls for the women. You see, pursued he, that by running from spaw to bathing-place, from bathing place to horse-race, and from horse-race to some spaw or bathing-place again, they may contrive to fill up their time tolerably well: and such is their love of change, that they even grow weary of the sameness of this world, and often send themselves out of it with a halter or a dose of poison.

These horse-races, continued he, are the constant causes of excessive gaming; and are particularly destructive to those who themselves keep running horses, from their immense expence.

Notwithstanding the bad effects of them in this country, according to our friend's account, I own (as a

Yorkshireman), that I had a very great partiality for that amusement, and had for some time resolved to see the first that happened at a reasonable distance from town, before we sailed; the time for which was fast approaching.

The winter Theatres were shut up soon after our arrival, and a summer one opened, which was also Royal. Aristopharis was the patentee of it; a very extraordinary character! he had wrote a great number of comedies, full of wit and humour; but as they were all on temporary subjects, they probably will not long survive him, unless he or somebody else writes a very full commentary on his works. In the mean time they answered his purpose of bringing him full houses.

None

None but his own pieces are almoſt ever performed at his houſe. He is alſo an excellent companion, and much ſought after by the Nomras and men of wit; giving in his turn, elegant and expenſive entertainments. He has ſpent two or three fortunes, beſides the immenſe ſums he has raiſed on the public; being in that reſpect a perfect contraſt to Garrimond.

We ſometimes made parties to go to that Theatre, and when we could, carried ſome of the Bonhommican ladies of the factory with us ; but it was not often we could prevail with them, as they ſtill retained their own country manners ; having (to comply with the faſhion only) got ſmall artificial head-wings. Ariſtopharis

pharis always played the principal characters in his own pieces, and frequently mimicked the person and manner of the culprit intended to be expofed to public ridicule, in fo excellent a manner, that the whole audience were kept in a continual roar.

In fhort, this theatre might be called by way of excellence, the laughing theatre; there was no forbearing. I do not believe a perfon brought directly from the fabled cave of Trophonius could have refifted,

We had not yet been at Rondelleva or Fairy-hall, but now made parties for both; not in the fame evening as many people do; we hufbanded

our

our amufements better than that came to. With much perfuafion fome of our ladies accompanied us to the former, but nothing could draw them to the latter. Rondelleva is a vaft rotund (in fize far exceeding the Theo-pan), about a mile from town. It really ftruck us very much at our firft entrance. The company is as great a mixture as can well be imagined; from the Prince and Princefs of the blood royal, to any body who can appear in a decent drefs, and pay half an ecuris for entrance. It may properly be called an immenfe Coffee-houfe for both. fexes. Every thing is however decent at this place, even the Alæ-putas conceal their wings as much as they poffibly can. There is always a band of mufic, and fome fingers; but no body feemed to mind them. The place was exceedingly crouded that night, and however agreeable it may be at other times, it certainly was much the reverfe on this occafion.

The entertainment at this place, is to walk round the room, and round the room, like a horfe in a mill. You fee but half the company, for you muft ftill follow your leaders; (this is occafioned by a large fupport to the roof in the center of the room, in which there is a fire in cold weather); fhould any number pretend to go the oppofite way, there would be a full ftop. The only method of feeing the whole, is to take poffeffion of a box (if you can, for on thefe crouded nights there are great demands for them); fit down in it, and
fee

fee all the company pafs you at your eafe. You have Tea and Coffee for your half ecuris if you chufe it.

On crouded nights it is very difficult to get to your carriages; fo much fo, that company are often kept till three or four in the morning folely on that account. To prevent which, and our curiofity being fatisfied, we made our retreat a little after eleven, and happily got fafe home.

We were all men in the Fairy-hall party, and certainly it is well named; for every thing looks like Fairy-land or enchantment. A large garden well laid out, interfperfed with elegant buildings; in the midft of which, is one for a band of mufic and good voices. Statues, Paintings, Cafcades
ftrike

strike your eyes, whatever side you turn to. The whole illuminated with some thousands of globular lamps, which make it almost as light as day. What added much to the oddity of the scene (though it was a great nuisance), was the Alæ-putas flying about in great numbers, and perching upon the trees in a ridiculous manner; calling to the men as they walked past, and inviting them up to them. You pay but a scheris entrance, but the proprietor has great profit on his meat and wine, as it is customary to sup here. We were resolved to see the whole of the place, and went into a box. The prices of every thing are fixed; so much for a chicken, so much for a slice of beef, &c. &c. &c. The provisions, though dear, were good of their kind; but the high priced wines were execrable. You sit in open boxes, exposed to the ribaldry of the Alæ-putas and drunken apprentices; who, after ten o'clock, became very noisy and quarrelsome. They soon became too much so, for us to have any satisfaction in a longer stay; we therefore paid our bill and went home, wishing we had done it sooner.

I have already mentioned my predilection for a horse-race, luckily those of Epicem (a small town, fifteen miles from the capital) were advertised; and as none of the commanders had ever seen one, they were the more easily persuaded to go one of the days. Fortunately the weather was favourable, and brought a vast deal

deal of company on the downs. They were of all forts; a great number of handfome carriages filled with Comras and Comrinas; fome Nomras and Nomrinas; crouds of horfemen of all ranks; and not a few Alæ-putas in high life, in their carrs and fix.

The running horfes feemed not inferior to ours in England; they were indeed beautiful creatures, and it warmed my heart to look at them.

They ftarted, and every body (efpecially thofe who betted) were in an agitation of fpirits; galloping about, and offering betts, at every feeming alteration in their progrefs.

The carrs and fix attended them in the air, which had a beautiful effect. At laft the pufh was made, the

the horses strained every nerve, and the Riders spared neither whip nor spur to urge them on. Of the four that run, two kept so near a-breast, it could not be distingushed which was foremost; then the noise was loud, and betts altered every moment, in favour now of one, now of another; at last they reached the winning post, and by the exertion of the rider one of them gave a spring forward, and won by half a neck. Nothing but shouting and hollowing was then to be heard; some glorying in their judgment, others cursing their ill-luck, and accusing the losing Rider of being bribed.

I shall not tire my reader with a description of the other heats; suffice it to say, that the sport was as fine as as ever I faw in England. We had alfo a Chafe which very much diverted the company, and was quite unexpected. One of the Carr-born Goddeffes, had very wifely trained fix Falcons for her equipage, and came with them to the ground that day, for the firft time of trying them in public. Another was drawn by fix beautiful Pigeons, which the Falcons unluckily got a view of; away they flew after them, being very little under command of their Charioteer. The Pigeons exerted themfelves with all their ftrength to efcape their enemy, nor did their Goddefs reftrain them. The efforts on both fides were great, and the chafe long, fometimes in one direction, and fometimes in another; at laft, from the great agitation, both the Goddeffes were

were thrown from their Carrs, the reins and harnefs were broke, and the poor Pigeons devoured. To put my reader out of pain for the Goddeffes, I have the pleafure to affure him they got no hurt, as their large fpreading wings fupported them in the air and broke the fall. We returned to town very well fatisfied with our diverfion, and had the luck to efcape being robbed.

CHAP. IX.

Every thing prepared for failing. Take leave at Court; and of our Friends. Sail with a fair wind. Speak with some Armoserian Privateers. A Storm. Meet with a Dutch Frigate. The Captain of her gives the Author a passage to Battavia. Tender parting with Moraveres. His friendly behaviour to the Author; and humanity to the Dutch Crew. The Scurvy abates on board the Harlem Frigate, from the use of Malt and other things Moraveres spared them. Arrives at Battavia. Sent for by the Governor and Council, to interrogate him concerning the Island of Bonhommica. Ships fitted out for that discovery. The Author falls sick, but recovers. Sails to the Cape in a Dutch Indiaman. Gets a passage home in an English one. Arrives in Old England.

EVERY thing was now ready for failing, and we only waited for a fair a fair wind. We took leave at Court, of the Ambaſſador, and of the Nomras who had ſhewed us civilities; but with much more real concern of the worthy Merchants of the factory, and of the virtuous Bonaris. Our grief at parting would have been greater, if we had not hoped to meet again the next year, or at leaſt to hear from one another. The wind came fair the day after we lay on board, and we ſailed the 1ſt of February 1776, having been near three months in this famous capital.

Our voyage was proſperous and agreeable during the whole month of February, and moſt part of that of March; no occurrence happened worth mentioning, except that we met, and ſpoke with ſeveral Armoſerian Privateers;

Privateers; who paid due honours to the Bonhommican flag, feeing us so well prepared for them; or what is more probable, having no defign to make themfelves any new enemies.

The goodnefs of heart which Moraveres fhewed on every occafion, made me almoft adore him; and I perceived that my endeavours to imitate their manners, had not been entirely without fuccefs, as I gained ground daily in his affections. The orderly behaviour of the inferior officers and common failors, was alfo truly admirable; and I often ufed to make the comparifon in my own mind, betwixt them and our Englifh crews, where nothing is done without

out bawling, curfing, and fwearing in a moft fhameful manner.

On March 27th, when by our reckoning we were within a hundred leagues of Bonhommica, and were happy in the thoughts of foon feeing our friends; at 2 p. m. the wind, which had moftly been at weft, changed to S. W. and frefhened confiderably. This obliged us to take in our top-gallant-fails, and even to reef the top-fails. At half after four we took them in alfo, and at fix reefed our courfes. Thus we run all that night, but the gale ftill increafed upon us. In the morning we counted our whole convoy ftill in company, and put in another reef in our courfes. On the evening of the 28th, the Quadarow made the fignal for lying to

under a reefed mizen, for fear of shooting ahead of our port. It blew a perfect storm all night, and the ship pitched so dreadfully, that we had some apprehensions of her foundering. On the 29th at day-break, not one of the fleet was to be seen; and the storm instead of abating grew every hour more violent; so that to prevent her foundering, we were obliged to put her before the wind under a treble reefed foresail. She did not now labour in the sea as before, but went with a prodigious velocity; at least nine or ten knots an hour as well as we could judge, heaving the log-line in so mountainous a sea being impracticable; however, on the 30th, we found it necessary to take in also the foresail, and let her drive under bare poles. Moraveres

veres was as composed in this tempest as at other times, giving me his opinion and orders with the coolness of a virtuous man, who was prepared for all events. Nor did he even at such a time overlook the firmness with which the masts and rigging bore the buffeting of the winds, to the honour of British improvements.

This storm continued with unabated violence to April 9th, when it began to lose somewhat of its fury; but went off gradually as it came on. The 10th it abated considerably, but a prodigious high sea still run.

We now got out some sails, and altered our course for Bonhommica. On the 11th fair weather, and the sea much fallen: had at noon an observation, fervation, and found ourfelves in 10° 52' fouth latitude, and by feveral diftances of the fun and moon in 152° 34' eaft longitude. At 2 p. m. faw a fail which we concluded muft be one of the convoy, fhe was to leeward, fo we bore down to her; but how great was my furprife and joy when we neared her, to difcover fhe was European built and feemed to be Dutch. I acquainted Moraveres with it, who faid, it would give him great pleafure to fee an European fhip, but was afraid it would be the means of depriving them of me; however, faid he, we muft put away all felfifhnefs from our hearts, when the happinefs of our friends is concerned.

A boat was immediately hoifted out, and the Dutchman feeing we intended

intended coming on board of him, ordered the ſhip to lie to for us, and the Ardefow was commanded to do the ſame. We went on board, and found her a frigate of 22 guns called the Harlem, and commanded by John Van Trump. I had much ado to make myſelf underſtood by the Captain, as he was maſter of neither Engliſh nor French, nor I of Dutch. The ſailors being all on deck out of curioſity to ſee ſuch outlandiſh people, I aſked in Engliſh, if none of them were Engliſhmen; they all ſhook their heads. I then ſpoke to the ſame purpoſe in French, when one came forward, and ſaid in that language that he was a Walloon. The Captain was a well looking man, and polite, for his country. He aſked us very civilly into his
cabbin,

cabbin, where the Walloon attended us. When there, he begged the favour to know how I came into thefe feas, and more particularly in a fhip, and with people, whom he had never feen, or heard any thing fpoke of. That all Europe believed, that there was no civilifed nation in that part of the globe; but by the conftruction of the fhip, its large fize, and the appearance of the people, it feemed to be otherwife. I gave him a faithful account of my travels, and particularly of the Ifland of Bonhommica, and its inhabitants, giving them the due praife their virtues deferved; letting him know alfo, that I had entered into their fervice, as there feemed little probability of my ever getting back to my own dear country.

try. I however had done it with this expreſs reſervation, that I was at liberty to quit it upon any occaſion of meeting with a European ſhip, that would carry me thither. But though I told him nothing but truth, no mention was made of the ſouthern continent; that great diſcovery I reſerved for my dear countrymen. I now in return requeſted an account of his buſineſs in theſe ſeas, but found him very reſerved on that ſubject. He only ſaid, that he had been ſent out by the governor general and council of Batavia, on a voyage of diſcovery; that he had been at New-Zealand, where one of his boat's crews had been cut off, and devoured by the ſavages; and that having been already out fifteen months, with a very ſickly ſhip's company, he was

returning

returning thither with all poſſible expedition, before the ſcurvy had quite diſabled them. He concluded with offering me in a very handſome manner, a paſſage to Batavia, which I accepted with great thankfulneſs. He aſked us to ſtay dinner with him, which the Quadarow conſented to, on condition he dined with him next day, on board the Ardefow. This he readily conſented to, having no doubt a curioſity to ſee the ſhip, and the manners of the people who navigated her. Before dinner Captain Van Trump ſhowed Moraveres every part of the Harlem, who was not ſo much pleaſed as might have been expected; but Dutch ſhips are in general of a clumſy and heavy conſtruction in compariſon with the Engliſh.

The

The Dutch Captain gave us the beft dinner that was in his power; every thing was neat and plain, which greatly pleafed our Quadarow. What we wanted in frefh meat, he made up in good liquors; arrack punch and Conftantia wine, were both quite new to Moraveres, and much admired by him. After dinner, we returned to the Ardefow (which I fhall no longer call our fhip, as I was fo foon to leave her), and I began to put my affairs in fome order, to be removed on board the Harlem. I muft honeftly own, that though I had now a profpect of feeing Old England again, which I had for a long time almoft defpaired of ; yet the parting with Moraveres, and the thoughts of never feeing my royal miftrefs or any of my friends in Ludorow more, ftruggled hard

hard in my thoughts, with the love of my native country; and it was not an eafy conqueft which the latter at laft gained. Moraveres obferved my concern, and was pleafed with it; he faid it fhewed a good heart, not to quit people who valued me, without regret, though it was to return to my own country. But, continued he, you muft endeavour to fhake it off, as you are only doing your duty, and I fhall comfort myfelf in your abfence with the hopes of your being happy, and that you will not entirely forget me and my country.

He then made fome inquiries concerning the Dutch nation; and when I had given him an account of their fmall territory in Europe, and their extenfive commerce, together with their great power in India; their character,

character, manners, &c. &c. He said, they were a singular instance of the powerful effects of commerce, but there were some things in their character which he could not approve of; they seem, said he, a selfish people, and make every thing give way to that sordid principle. I afterwards (at his own desire) informed him in what manner I was to get home; and he (understanding, that after reaching Batavia, a long voyage was to be made to Europe) went to his desk, and brought out a purse filled with 200 Tudarines, and said to me, Bowman, you are going amongst a selfish people, where you will be an intire stranger; if you cannot amongst men of that character pay for what you want, you will be very ill served. Receive then this money which I have no occasion for, it may be of use to you. I was delighted, and yet hurt with the generosity of my friend, and would have excused myself from accepting it, by letting him know, that I was not without money enough (I hoped) to serve my occasions; but finding he would take my refusal very ill, I was obliged to acquiesce. I wrote a letter to the Lurgow Amorow, begging he would acquaint her Majesty with my great acknowledgments and gratitude for all her favours, which I assured him would never be obliterated from my memory, while I had life; and also assuring him of my great respect and regard for his own person and virtues, as well as for the whole Bonhommican nation. I wrote also to my host Lurgofage, inclosing one in it to my dear friend Ouragow at Seripante.

Next

Next day, Captain Van Trump came on board according to promise, and brought his interpreter with him. Before dinner I shewed him the ship, which was cleared for that purpose, and he was not a little surprised with it; but as I honestly told him how she had been fitted out under my directions, by order of her Bonhommican Majesty, his admiration was somewhat lessened. He got the best dinner that the ship could afford, and wine both of the growth of Bonhommica and Luxo-volupto; which were very different from any he ever drank, and consequently increased his wonder. Conversing about Bonhommica, the Captain said to me, that it seemed impossible to him, that an Island of so large a size, and lying in the longitude and latitude I had mentioned, should hitherto have escaped

caped difcovery; but, on confidering the vaft extent of the Pacific Ocean, it by chance might happen; and what he faw before him, and all around, was a plain proof that it had.

In viewing the fhip, he had obferved that all the men looked in perfect health, without the leaft appearance of the fcurvy, and at dinner mentioned it to me as fomething very uncommon. I anfwered him, that we had only been feventy days out of port, which was not fo long, but with common management that diftemper might be prevented; for I affured him the two Britifh fhips which have lately been in thefe feas, had been 117 days without feeing land; and yet to my knowledge without any appearance of it. He begged to know, in what manner they were victualled,

victualled, or if any other means were used to prevent that destructive malady. Upon this, I gave him a full account of our provision and management (but with which I shall not trouble the reader), and afterwards told him that the Ardefow had by way of experiment been conducted exactly in the same manner; which probably had contributed to the healthfulness of the men. After sitting silent for a minute or two, he replied, that I had told him of a very happy discovery, and wished he had an opportunity of trying it upon his sickly crew. To which I rejoined, that Moraveres was so humane and worthy a man, that I was certain if there was such a quantity left, as to allow any to be spared, that he would readily do it. The worthy Quadarow, upon being told of the fickly condition of the Dutch fhip, and what was requefted of him, immediately fent for a return of thefe ftores to be made him; and finding he fafely might fpare a part to people in fuch diftrefs, ordered a certain quantity of each to be properly cafked up and put into the Harlem's boat.

Van Trump expreffed his acknowledgments for his humanity, and it being now time to depart, I took a laft farewel of my dear friend, which was on neither fide with dry eyes; and alfo of the quarter-deck officers; even the common men were not forgot; and I have the fatisfaction of remembering, that they all fhowed a concern at parting with me.

The fhips fteering different courfes, were foon out of fight of each other; but

but my heart ſtill glowed with the remembrance of the Ardefow and her excellent commander.

Captain Van Trump treated me very well during our voyage to Batavia, and the favour I had obtained for his ſick men required no leſs at his hands. By the help of our interpreter, I gave the ſurgeon inſtructions how the ſtores were to be managed to the beſt advantage, and being an idle man, even overlooked the giving of them regularly myſelf. It was with infinite pleaſure that I obſerved their ſalutary effects; thoſe who were only beginning to be ill, recovered in a very ſhort time; and thoſe who had been long down, grew by degrees better and better.

The Dutch language does not differ greatly from the Engliſh; I took ſome

some pains in acquiring it while on board this ship, and not altogether without success; before we got to Batavia, I could talk it tolerably well. We arrived at this famous Emporium June 26th, 1776, without any thing worth relating having happened in the voyage.

Before I had been a week at Batavia, a very civil message was sent me from the Governor-general and Council, desiring to see me, which I accordingly obeyed. When I was introduced, it soon appeared what their business with me was, by the Governor's immediately interrogating me, concerning the ship from which the Harlem had taken me. I gave him a faithful account as far as it went, of the Island of Bonhommica and every thing I knew concerning it, with which they seemed satisfied, as it agreed exactly with Van Trump's account of the Ardefow, and her ship's company. Before I left Batavia, two ships were fitting out to go on that discovery; whereof one was to be commanded by Van Trump. This gave me some uneasiness, as I wished no body might get the start of my own dear countrymen, in an intercourse with so virtuous a people; and I hope they will do me the justice to consider, that, circumstanced as I was, it was utterly impossible for me to conceal that valuable discovery from the Dutch.

I had hitherto enjoyed an uninterrupted good state of health during all my dangers and fatigues; but the stinking putrid air of this abominable place, was too powerful for me. I fell down in a putrid fever, and was

many

many days ſtruggling for life. The moſt noted phyſicians were called to my aſſiſtance by Van Trump, who, to do him juſtice, acted a friendly part by me; and at the end of three weeks (whether from the medicines I had taken, or from youth and a good conſtitution, I ſhall not determine), my difeaſe took a favourable turn. I began to recover, but it was very ſlowly; which no doubt was in a great meaſure occaſioned by my continuing in the ſame bad air. My deſire of being removed into the country was complied with; and I found great benefit by that change. Sickneſs, it is generally ſaid, is chargeable; this I found to my coſt; for had it not been for my good friend's purſe of Tudorines, I could not have defrayed the expences of mine. I got Dutch money for them from a gold-a goldsmith; and many of the Merchants and Council bought them from him as great curiosities.

Van Trump undertook to procure me a passage, in the first ship bound to the Cape of Good-Hope; and to acquaint me when she was ready to sail. This did not happen till the middle of October, when I came to town, and went on board immediately, after thanking the Captain for all his favours. The ship was a Dutch East Indiaman, called the Oster-hought, commanded by Isaac Van Neck, a very sensible good sort of man. As soon as we got out to sea, I found myself quite a different man, and daily recovered my strength and spirits. We had rather a tedious passage to the Cape, though no very bad weather; having sailed from Batavia the

the end of October, and not arriving there till the beginning of March 1777. I was now got to a known country, and went to lodge at the fame houfe I had been well treated at, four years and a half before. Englifh company's fhips were frequently coming from India, and calling here for refrefhments in their way to Europe. I took my paffage home in the Triton, the Hon. Captain Elphinfton commander, a moft agreeable and worthy man, who made every one on board his fhip happy. We called at St. Helena, as is ufual for the company's fhips, but made no long ftay, had a profperous voyage home, and came to an anchor in the Downs, on the 24th of July; when I foon had the happinefs of breathing my native air, of finding my dear father in health,

health, and all my family and relations very happily eftablifhed.

The only lofs I had to regret, was that of Sir Charles Saunders; him I moft fincerely lamented, both as a worthy man, and the only patron I had in the Britifh navy. I have an ambition to ferve my King and Country, and defire no other reward for my great difcoveries, than to be admitted to the fame rank which I left in the Bonhommican fervice. But as in this country every thing goes by intereft, I almoft defpair of fuccefs; and heartily wifh my good friend Omai was ftill here, who, I make no doubt, would have exerted to the utmoft, all his intereft with the Great in my favour.

It requires no nice inveftigation to difcover, that the Britifh manners at prefent present resemble much more those of the Luxo-voluptans, than the Bonhommicans. I am sorry to find it so, but for my own part I shall endeavour to form my friendships with those only, who have the greatest similitude to the latter nation; whose virtuous lives shall be the models for my imitation.

As the opportunity of returning to my native country was so unexpected, and happened at sea; there was no possibility of bringing any specimens of the manufactures, arms, or curiosities of the countries I visited, with me. However, if any gentleman will give himself the trouble of calling at my lodgings in St. Alban's-Street, I can shew him the coins of Bonhommica and Luxo-volupto; and some of the manufactures of both countries

in

in my Bonhommican uniform, and the cloaths I made up at Miro-volante to appear in at court.

I have not increased the size and price of this small volume, by a vocabulary of words, which I could easily have furnished from the languages I acquired. But if the Public shews any curiosity concerning these languages, they shall be indulged with something more complete than has hitherto appeared, of those spoke in the southern hemisphere; which I shall publish by subscription.

Thus have I, without any expence to my country, discovered the hitherto supposed, but much doubted of, Great Southern Continent. A fifth division of this Terraqueous Globe, of no inconsiderable magnitude; being (by the

the best information I could obtain) at least as large as Europe. And I hope from the known generosity of my countrymen, that I shall not be so ungratefully used by them, as the great Columbus was by the Spaniards; but that they will do me the honour of giving my name to it; which I think without dispute I have a much better right to, than Americus Vesputius had to that of America.

I shall not pretend to dictate to the Public, by which of my names it should be called, either of them is at their service; but if they will allow me to give my opinion, I think BOWMANIA would be softer, and more in unison with the names of the other divisions so long in use, than HILDEBRANDIA.

F I N I S.

www.ingramcontent.com/pod-product-compliance
Lightning Source LLC
Chambersburg PA
CBHW030553300426
44111CB00009B/958